HER HIKE

A MEMOIR

WRITTEN BY
JESSICA RYAN CHENARD

ISBN: 979-8-9862453-0-0
LCCN: 2022910022

Printed in the United States of America

To my brother, Richard,
who gave me my North Star.
Without a shadow of a doubt
you guided me to write our story.

Prologue

I wanted to see Richard. I also knew that seeing him would break me. My parents let me make my own decision about going to see him. With my head bowed and my chin digging into my collar bone, I avoided eye contact and silently pleaded, *Make the decision for me.* They were in no state to do so, and I knew that they too were already broken.

The last time I had the option to see Richard, he was in the morgue. My dad had warned me that they hadn't been able to cover the bruising, and I would see it if I went. Because of this, I chose not to go. I wish they would have just forbidden me.

~

Not even forty-eight hours prior, my dad had called me and said he was in front of my house. The house I lived in during college was only thirty minutes away from my parents' house.

My heart sunk to my feet—it was not like him to show up unannounced. I asked him why, and he told me he just needed me to come outside. I rushed out the door, leaving it wide open, and saw my dad standing on the walkway that was overgrown with grass and weeds, the car headlights silhouetting him. My uncle was just behind him, walking up the path, and I noted how odd it was that they were there together in that very moment.

It was 9 p.m. No, maybe 10 p.m. I'm not really sure; time meant nothing in that moment, and a lump had started to form in my throat. My dad stretched his arms out around me, pulled me into his embrace, and said, "There's been an awful accident with Richard."

Already burrowed into his shoulder, trying to protect myself from the words, I asked, "Is he okay?" I could already feel the impact of the answer I instantly suspected.

"No, he's not," my dad uttered. He never said Richard had died, sparing me the pain of hearing those two words come from his mouth, but I knew.

My dad asked if I could pack some clothes because my mother desperately needed me. He told me that she was back at my aunt's house with her and my two cousins. I heard my uncle tell my roommate vaguely what had happened as my dad and I walked down the hallway to my room. Within a few seconds, she was already on the phone relaying the news to my best friend, Nicole.

My room was a mess, clothes and textbooks everywhere, my bed unmade. My dad stood in the center of it all and stared around at the clutter. Looking back, I imagine that the chaos of my room was a reflection of what he was feeling at that moment. The chaos circling all around him was a mirror he did not want to acknowledge. He let out a sob like I had never heard before. I hugged him tightly, then proceeded to throw items I didn't even look at into a bookbag. Anything to get him out of this reflection.

I was ready. But truthfully, nothing I could have packed would have prepared me for the next several days.

~

I thought back to all of this while my Aunt Misty and cousin Tommy perused the aisles of Target with me two days later. They'd brought me here to get me out of the house so I wasn't alone while my parents went to see Richard. I picked up items and put them back down. With flicks of my wrist, I swiped through all of the white plastic hangers on one clothing rack, and then another, never looking at the items that hung on them. I didn't feel present in those aisles, but my aunt and cousin did their best to distract me. Tommy pulled an obnoxious beanie with bear ears on his head as one of his distraction techniques, and I forced a laugh to show them both that they were doing a good job.

Aunt Misty had also taken me to dinner at Ruby Tuesday after my grandma passed away almost a decade prior. My grandma had lived with us at the time, and my parents didn't want me seeing the mortician take her away. I'd ordered a broccoli cheese soup, and after two of the most disgusting bites I've ever swallowed, I spent what felt like hours twirling my spoon around in the hardening broth. I'd gone to bed at my aunt's house, barely slept, and my stomach howled through the night.

This time, it was Target. I vaguely remember buying a pair of jeans, deciding I hadn't packed enough from my college house, even though it was only thirty minutes away from home. I would not be driving out there by myself anytime soon. Driving and being alone seemed foreign, even somewhat impossible. The jeans were too wide and draped over my legs like two blankets. I cannot recall ever wearing them after I purchased them.

~

The day after Richard died, the house was swarmed by friends and family. I didn't mind all the visitors. I didn't want to be alone. Somehow, people sharing their condolences and spending time with us made the truth feel less real than the still and quiet of being alone. Solitude was when the nightmare felt real; that's when the walls came closing in on me.

Even though I enjoyed the visitors, sometimes I would need a break. I would excuse myself and walk down the hallway to the bathroom. Rarely did I actually need to use the bathroom. I was just in desperate need of a door to close behind me for a few minutes so I could exist in a space where eyes were not fixated on me.

Whenever I walked down the hallway, I would glance over to the long wall. Some of our childhood photos had once been proudly displayed in a collage that I'd created for our mother as a gift years prior. But on that day, the photos were not the same as what I had once placed there. I ran my fingers over frames from which photos were missing. Some photographs had had pieces cut out and then had been placed back in their designated spots. As I traced the empty frames with my finger, tears formed in the corners of my eyes because I knew that Richard had done this to them. Richard had carefully removed himself from photos or trashed them altogether. This clue indicated when he started to become a shell of himself. I would walk down the hallway, touching the vacancies, and wish over every bare space that he would somehow understand, wherever he was, that he was still good.

In early November 2011, my older brother, Richard, took his own life. After a several-year addiction to Adderall, increased prescription dosages, and mistreatment by medical professionals, my brother lost his battle. After my parents pleaded with the doctors to listen, to consider what they were telling them, one finally listened and acted in an astronomically erroneous way. Out of fear for his career and not for my brother's life, he cut my brother off completely and suddenly. Richard was forced to quit cold turkey after months of taking an exorbitantly high dosage. Before that, whenever the pills ran out, as they often did, doctors would always place another slip of Rx paper into Richard's shaking hand. This time, there was no piece of paper. His hands did not calm; there was no temporary fix. This sent him into a spiral, and he plummeted mentally and physically into a withdrawal that he would never come back from.

His story is well known through a front-page article in *The New York Times* titled: "Drowned in a Stream of Prescriptions," written by Allan Schwarz. It was published on February 3, 2013. If you Google this and read, the first three paragraphs alone perfectly summarize the worst time in my life. Those paragraphs were the tip of the iceberg, and I've chosen to let inquiring minds read about that iceberg through that article. But Richard's story—his life—deserves so much more. That's why, one day, I began writing. At first, not expecting to compile an entire book, I simply wanted to share who my brother really was with the world.

Abusing Adderall changed every aspect of Richard. He went from someone with a bright personality and excellent social skills to secluding himself and pushing us away. He went from someone who wanted to help and motivate others to someone who denied anything good being left within him. I remember who Richard was, and more importantly, who he could have become. In a world where he no longer exists, I want his memory to be alive. I want his story to run rampant and to do the most good it could, because his story didn't end the day he lost his battle. He passed the baton to me, and although it took years, I eventually became ready to share the truest version of him, which I still know and love to this day.

My parents have appeared on *The Today Show* and *Dr. Oz.* They have offered up their perspective on what happened to Richard in documentaries and in front of medical boards. All of this was an effort to help prevent what happened to their son from happening to someone else.

In November 2011, I had no clue how to start picking up the pieces of this shattered life he'd left us in the wake of his demise, and it took me years to figure it out. The story of what happened to Richard is well known. But this is my story of what I made of his loss, the lesser-known story that society rarely hears. This story is where life continues after the online comments stop, after the cameras and reporters go away, after the lawyers are done for the day.

This is the story of how I journeyed to keep Richard's memory alive. This is how I have chosen to introduce the world to the other side of him. This is how, picking up the pieces, I tape the torn pictures back together and dedicate my words to showing that he is still good. This is me remembering him before the pills, remembering the Richard that he himself could not remember. This is the story of how I healed.

CHAPTER 1

Her

Slowly, she starts to hike. Then suddenly, she flocks to trails and mountains. Waterfalls, wildflowers, and valleys become her refuge. Butterflies, rain showers, and rainbows begin to console her.

Sweat drips off her nose and earlobes as she reaches a summit, step after repetitive step up the trail. Breathing in deeply and exhaling loudly, she feels as if her heart will beat out of her chest, afraid that it wants to jump out and sit on a cool rock and wave as she passes it by. No matter the threat of leaving, of jumping, of beating from her chest and then into her throat, her heart always stays, time and time again reassuring her what her mind and body are truly capable of.

Reminding me what I'm capable of, because "she" is me. I am her.

I'm fresh, full of energy, and making great strides. I hike down, down, down to the waterfall, and except for a little wear on my knees, it's easy in the beginning. I sometimes forget to think about the return hike that begins once I'm at the base of the waterfall.

Usually I want the hard work at the beginning, so I know I'm working toward a reward. Facing the beginning of something that's going to be hard, I want to know that I'll be able to lead myself up and out of it with or without a fight.

But with waterfalls, the hike back up is where the hard work comes in. I see the waterfall; I put my feet in the cool mountain spring, listening to the water rush by me. I sit next to the rock wall with wildflowers poking out of every crevice where they're able to grow their roots. Bright yellows and oranges of flower petals billow up and out of the cracks along the wall, all to offer a safe place for a butterfly to land. And dozens of butterflies flutter about, drinking water from the mist of the waterfall that blankets the flowers.

The bliss of the waterfall is truly the pinnacle point. It's a beacon of hope when I've hiked down and realized that I will have to hike up. It's where the grit comes in; it's where my character develops. My favorite hikes are to waterfalls because I experience the miracle in the middle, giving me the strength to continue my journey. And in my experience, the middle is where miracles truly are in life.

~

I did not wake up the morning after my brother passed away and witness any miracles. I did not say to myself, "I am going to be an avid hiker." No, I woke up in the low glow of morning light peeking through the blinds at my parents' house, and for a millisecond, I forgot what had happened the night before. I forgot that I was truly still trapped in an avalanche, not knowing which way was out.

That is, until I heard the sobs of my mother seeping through the walls. Like a search and rescue dog pawing at the snow to show where a human is trapped, my mother's sounds of grief alerted me and brought me to the surface. I resurfaced uneasily, pulling my covers down to expose my face, and the air outside smacked me with a dose of reality. I wondered how different or similar I would feel if I was being dragged to the snow's surface after an avalanche.

Still, I got up out of the covers, despite knowing that their warmth was the only thing that physically guarded me from reality that morning, and I opened the door to the hallway. Empty photo frames in the hallway encountered me first, like a billboard advertising that the world was a new, foreign, and more terrifying world than the one I'd woken up to the morning before.

Photographs of Richard used to be there, ones with us as children together. There was one that depicted him sitting in the snow at Big Sky with my parents, arms wrapped around each other. The frames were empty, but like a photographic memory, my mind protected me and helped me see the photos there. My memories helped the billboard advertisements give me a glimmer of hope. A hint that his story was not over. A hint that I did in fact have far to go, but more importantly, that I had somewhere to go.

I would one day face all of this on mountains, and I would be able to tell myself that it was time to heal.

But first, in my parents' house the day after I found out that my brother died, I had to lift my feet and take one of the hardest paths I'd ever embarked on. I managed to turn to the right onto the carpet in our hallway, walking down to my parents' bedroom. My knees bent as I got into bed behind my mom and lay beside her, my arm draping over her side. The hike up had begun. Even though we were stagnant, frozen there for a while, this was our first step in our journey.

Though my future path was unknown that morning, as I lay in my mother's bed, I reminded myself that Richard's story did not have to end there. And although I could not see any of the trails that I would eventually take, I knew in my beating heart, the heart that did not leave me, the heart that pounded in my chest, that my part of the story was just beginning.

CHAPTER 2

Maps

"Ryan, you would love the places I've been to, hiking and camping. You come across waterfalls suddenly and—well, you would need to bring your camera. You would love taking pictures if you went with me.... You really should go with me sometime. You would love it."

I remember this fast-paced conversation like it was yesterday and like it was years ago at the same time. How Richard's sentences, his broken fragments, carried only the slightest pauses between them.

When he mentioned that I should go hiking and camping with him, it was not much of an invitation at the time. He was always leaving unexpectedly to travel to the mountains to hike and camp by himself, but his invitation seemed more like a memory of what could have been. I was grateful for any conversation with Richard, although they were often very one-sided. We did not have a lot of them during this period of our lives. So, I paused and listened to his frenetic sentences, savoring every word.

Anybody will tell you that my brother was brilliant. A biology major, he graduated with honors after holding a presidential scholarship. He was active, a baseball player all the way from T-ball to college level. He loved the outdoors and always had lots of camping gear in the trunk of his car. He stood at six-foot-three with dark brown hair. His deeply rich brown eyes mirrored his hair and complimented his ear-to-ear smile. To this day, it's one of the brightest smiles I've seen.

Deep inside of Richard, an avalanche gained momentum. He couldn't control his addiction to Adderall, let alone stop it.

Because of his avalanche, because of time, I never took him up on his invitation. I will always regret that I never got the chance to take those trips with him. His words about them will be with me my entire life.

He told me that the views were breathtaking and the waterfalls he came across unannounced while backpacking would stop him in his tracks. He would stand there and marvel up at them.

After his passing, I found myself being called to nature. In those first moments, it was tentative and cautious. Over the next several years, I would answer to it. I would learn to marvel.

I imagine that this was what my brother was trying to say: *Pay attention to the days that you marvel in.* I am thankful to have the conversation of what could have been to hold onto like it's a piece of him. I began to search nature for sights where all I could do was stop to marvel at them.

Shortly after our conversation about hiking, camping, and the waterfalls he loved to see, Richard went missing. Well, as much as an adult who took money out of his mother's bank account and simply left home can be missing. We didn't know much, but we *did* know that even though he had hurt my parents, he was hurting much more. His actions later that day proved that.

It all started when Richard drove his silver Jetta out of the bank parking lot and instantaneously felt awful about what he had just done. He drove back to our parents' home, his knuckles white, I imagine, as he gripped the steering wheel. He threw his Jetta into park and left it running in the middle of the driveway with his driver-side door wide open as he rushed into the house.

He would do this from time to time with his car, as if he had forgotten all about it. I remember coming home some of those times, turning his car off for him, and bringing the keys inside. I would find him asleep in his room, his Jetta long forgotten. Although on that day, I did not come home in time.

With no one home, I imagine that he threw his camping gear into his pack, then scanned the fridge and pantry, grabbing the food and water that he could muster up in a hurry. As he went to leave, he paused by the counter, fidgeting his hand in the back pocket of his jeans. Remorse washed over him. I can feel his mind in a whirl-wind, a war battling between himself and his addiction. I imagine his eyes watering, the kind where your eyesight becomes blurred, and he wiped away one tear trickling down his cheek. That one tear held so much anguish as he took out our mother's debit card, leaving the wad of cash in his pocket, and placed the card on the counter just before he headed out the door.

After some time had passed, my parents had a gut feeling some-thing was wrong. They checked their bank account and realized what had happened. It was not out of the question to assume something volatile would happen on any given day during this period of our lives, but this is where it became clear to us that he either was not coming back or did not plan to come back for a while.

Though we were terrified, I liked to picture Richard having an adventure, one that was fulfilling and made him decide to come back to us for a little while longer. His white knuckles gradually gained more color as he drove farther and farther away from his life. Once his grip had relaxed, he probably rolled his windows down, driving down highways with the golden light of the sunset warming his face. He might have taken his left hand and stuck it out the window into the wind. Aside from standing on top of a mountain, driving with the windows down with the sunlight warming your face and your hand out the window with no real destination is the freest someone can feel. "Free" is an interesting word; I hope Richard felt free, even if it was just for a few moments.

I can imagine Richard wide-eyed, his backpack strapped on, and his water canister hitting his side slightly as it dangled from his pack. He probably began his hikes without maps, unlike me. That is where we are different. I use my GPS to drive to a mountain, and I screenshot the list of directions and the trail of my hike in case I lose phone service. No, if Richard used anything, it would have been paper maps, like the antique ones he often checked out from the library. He would have a compass in his right pocket.

He was still missing when I found my mother crying in the kitchen one evening. Paralyzed with fear, she could barely speak, and all her body would let her do was cry. She eventually spoke: "I just … don't want … something bad … I just want him home."

As she said the word "home," a picture of Richard skiing as a child loosened from under a magnet on the refrigerator and drifted past my mom to the wood floor.

Our earth exploded in an instant. My mother's tears became waterfalls, and it felt like the ground was breaking beneath us. His photograph hitting the ground caused the biggest earthquake I thought I would ever experience.

Mom's cries were painful to hear. Her pain ricocheted off of me as she shouted, "Why did that picture fall? What is he doing? Why isn't he here? What did he do? Am I ever going to see him again? Oh God, why did that picture fall?"

I sprinted to the picture, picked it up, and felt its edges as I punched it back onto the refrigerator, placing a magnet on each corner. I grabbed my mom and threw her entire body into mine, my arms wrapping around her. Nothing I did here was delicate. I repeated over and over again, "It means nothing. He will come home. It means nothing." But truthfully, I was petrified, and it took everything in me not to become paralyzed with her.

I believe in signs like that, but I believe that we only receive beautiful ones from our loved ones. In our early twenties, we can expect people like our grandparents to pass away, but not my brother, who was only four years older than me. Not the brother who always had it together, the one I'd looked up to my entire life.

I could never cry in front of my mother because it broke my heart to see hers shattering. Her grief and worry flooded a room, and I was afraid that if I added mine, we would all have drowned in it. But the main reason I could not cry in front of her was that deep inside me I knew, but did not want to admit, that I could eventually be the one child she had left.

After a while, I excused myself to take a shower, where I did most of my crying. As I stepped into the steam and the noise of the shower, I released all of what I had been keeping in. I cried beneath the showerhead, water beating down to muffle my sobs. I had a vision of my brother that I prayed was just my imagination. I hoped it was my mind wandering and picturing the worst, just as my mother had done when his picture fell from the refrigerator.

I pictured him on top of a mountain. He'd hiked there during daylight and became mesmerized by the views. He loved the view beneath him, visually making his problems seem so far away and small. He decided to camp there, but when nightfall came, the weather became windy, and it all seemed too dark. I imagined Richard stepping to the edge and peering over, and as he pondered how he would begin to do better, if he could have done better, something told him to look up. As he did, he saw a sky full of stars, and then he realized that the night was not as dark as it had originally seemed. Picturing my mom and myself back in our kitchen, I realized that her cries created an earthquake that ricocheted throughout not only our lives, but Richard's too. I imagined that simultaneously, a gust of wind pushed Richard forcefully toward his tent and away from the edge. He fell to the ground, gripping the dirt between his fingers, and whispered, "Thank you." He may not have realized it, but these two words were meant for our mother, and they bore repeating to her over and over again: "Thank you."

My mother's pure anguish, devastation, and remnants of hope that she clung to as a mother exploded into the universe. They reached my brother on top of the mountain and pushed him to the ground. It was an act of love, one that transcends all understanding. The dirt between his fingers rooted him as he dug in. He remembered that he was connected to us through the dirt that he gripped so tightly. He was anchored by the Earth beneath him. He began to feel safe again.

Our father came home from his search up and down the Blue Ridge Mountains armed with Richard's picture. He looked exhausted. We all did, for that matter.

A few days later, Richard opened the front door and walked into our home as if nothing had happened.

Everyone wanted to hug, but it was as if we had forgotten how. I desperately wanted air. I decided to give Richard and my parents space as they all paced and battled in their minds how they were going to talk to each other.

Quickly, I realized that I did not simply want air; I *needed* air. Bursting through the front door, I noticed that Richard's silver Jetta was not in the driveway. It wasn't in the cul-de-sac. Next thing I knew, I was all the way down the street, walking out of our neighborhood in search of his car. Finally, I saw the silver shimmering in the sun across the street in a church parking lot. I picked up my pace, running over, looking for an answer. I cupped my hands around my eyes and pushed them against his car window to peer in. I saw all of the maps in a pile on his passenger seat, and from what parts of them I could see, I gathered that they were maps of the Blue Ridge Mountains and Tennessee.

"What happened to you?" I questioned out loud with no one around to answer me. Terror washed over me, like clouds gathering for a thunderstorm, as I wondered if he was battling with leaving again. But afterward, it seemed that for a time, the Earth repaired itself from our earthquake.

A list: new vehicle — camper conversion van, money for research/travel, historic sites, museums, campgrounds, specific books.

— excerpt from Richard's journal

CHAPTER 3

Open—Close—Open—Close

What is the first thing you think of when you wake up? What is your first thought when sun rays shine through the blinds in your window and settle on your eyelids? Your eyes flutter several times, letting the last few seconds of your dream play out in your mind before you open your eyes. Open. Close. Open. Close. Open. After your eyes connect with the sunlight a few times, you are greeted with the morning.

Have you thought your first thought? On one particular morning, as my eyes connected to the bright sun, my first thought was of my brother. That was not unusual. Richard was often in my thoughts. From the moment I woke up to the moment I went to sleep, I thought about him. I wondered what he was doing, what his day consisted of. Had he seen my parents? Had everything gone okay? Even though we were not in an ideal place with each other, he was a continuous thought of mine.

I never knew what that type of love was until his addiction and depression started. I never understood how anyone could be furious at someone and love them to an extent that there was no comparison to the fury. I never knew that love could last between two people while pushing and pulling at each other to ask for help, to offer help, and to attempt to understand one another. Love that could last through turmoil. To me, this gave love an entirely new meaning. Love is complicated for many more reasons than most people will ever have to endure. Love is being hurt and angry, but also being beside you at a moment's notice. Love was present in my far-too-few phone calls and personal conversations with Richard. The ones where he was present, wanting help, and our family who loved him was there.

This day was no different. But I found myself wondering, *How did we get here?* We had endured months and months of Richard and my parents fighting. Battling with getting him help, and him not understanding. Him telling us a doctor would not keep prescribing something that was bad for him. But as he swallowed the pills that supposedly would not hurt him, they seeped into his bloodstream, and his thoughts and actions grew irrational, reckless, and at times scary. I'd had enough of seeing the emotional pain in all of us.

Richard was sleeping in the room next to mine in the home we'd grown up in. He had been sleeping all day. He'd started a pattern of staying up for days and then crashing, sleeping for days on end. I sat with a few sheets of paper and a pen. I began to cry, and then I began to write. I cried until I could not form any more tears. I could barely see the words that I was writing down.

Once I was done writing, I had to decide if I was going to give my letter to Richard. *Do I take this chance? Will this make him come around?* After debating for several minutes, I almost threw the letter away in the plastic trashcan in my room. But then I realized that if I never reminded my brother how much I loved him and how much I wanted to help him, I would never forgive myself.

I walked away from the trashcan and found myself in the hallway, walking toward Richard's room. I did not knock because I knew he was sleeping. Wrapping my fingers around the doorknob, I decided that I would do one of two things: leave the letter on his nightstand and walk out quietly, or wake him up and let him know I wrote him a letter. Taking a big gulp to try to swallow the lump in my throat, I turned the knob and walked toward his bed in the dark. The only light, shining in from the doorway, illuminated his still face. I took a deep breath.

Resting my hand gently upon his shoulder, I uttered his name, "Richard. Richard. Can you wake up? I wrote you a letter."

"Yeah, what?" Richard said as he stirred in his bed.

"I wrote you a note.... You don't have to read it now, but I wanted to let you know I wrote you one." After a few seconds of silence, I spoke again. "I'll put it here." Placing the letter on his nightstand, I gently whispered, "Please read it sometime tonight. I'd love it if you talked to me afterward."

"Okay," Richard mumbled as he turned over.

"I love you." I turned to leave his room. My eyes teared up, and my heart began to race. The heaviness and sadness suddenly fell on top of me because saying those words to Richard felt foreign. I tried to escape the feeling of guilt, to escape his room, as fast as possible because the weight of those words, the knowledge that they were alien to us, was almost too much to endure.

I was almost all the way out of Richard's room when I heard him answer me: "I love you too. Thank you."

I closed his door and rested my head against the wall. On my twenty-first birthday, we had said "I love you" on the phone to each other. These were the only two times in all those years of turmoil that I remembered us saying that to each other.

The heaviness stayed with me. *What did I just do? Is this going to work? Is he going to offer to talk to me tonight, and what will our conversation be like?* My heart pounded in my chest as I paced in my small room, envisioning a lengthy talk with Richard about life, our childhood memories, his feelings, and our futures. In that moment, I envisioned us crying together, hugging and walking arm in arm out of his room into the family room. We'd look at each other with tears streaming down our faces and tell our parents that Richard wanted to seek help. I was going to help him reassure himself that he was a good person, people loved him, and he could get through it.

All I could think about was his future. He would get through this bump in the road, and he would have a wife and kids someday. I would be there for him when he started dating his future wife and when it came time to tell her about all of this. He would be scared that she would run, but she wouldn't. She would stay with him, and they would become stronger because of it. I had his entire future dreamed up, and I was eager to get it started.

But before all of that could occur, he had to sleep off another hour or so. I twiddled my thumbs and tried to distract myself while I anxiously watched for his bedroom light to turn on.

As the new hour approached, Richard finally woke up and invited me into his room. He was sitting up in his bed, his back resting against the wall. I sat down at his desk and swiveled the chair from side to side due to my nerves. When we started talking about the letter, I was hopeful, but Richard became more closed off. His anxiousness and frustration gradually seeped into our conversation, and he started tapping the back of his head against the wall.

I like to think that my brain is protecting me, because all I remember after that is my parents eventually joined the conversation. Shortly after that, I was overcome with emotion. I left. I called my best friend and asked if I could stay the night at her house.

Once I got there, I was emotionally and physically exhausted. I laid my head down on a pillow and I shut down. My eyes closed. My eyes opened. Closed. Opened. Closed. Then the light was gone, and I began to dream.

That night, I dreamt about getting another opportunity to try again.

Sun: (start) twilite | rise | transit | set | (end) twilite
Moon: set. Rise. Transit. Set. Rise.

—excerpt from Richard's journal

CHAPTER 4

Dream

I was rested. I felt at peace. Without warning, a large mountain range appeared, higher than I had ever seen before. There were infinite layers, piles of mountains, one behind the other as far as the eye could see. I wondered if they would go on forever. I wondered if they went past the horizon line, where the elements of the landscape seemed to mesh together like the background of a watercolor painting.

The mountains directly in front of me were their own natural artwork, bare rock face and breathtakingly steep peaks. A blunt tree line separated the peaks from the bottom half of the mountains. There are patches of snow in various crevices, growing more common as my eyes traced the snow up to the peak of the mountain. The peaks came to abrupt points, and it seemed as if someone had taken sheets of snow and layered them on, covering the summit magnificently.

I thought to myself, *Maybe this was God, or maybe this was Richard, or maybe they both did this together... but would they have done all of this for me?*

I started to hike toward those mountains, and as I did, a crystal blue lake appeared at the foot of the mountain. There was a wooden picnic table just before the lake, the kind you'd see at a state park campsite, and I proceeded to walk down to it. I sat on top of the table with my back to the path I'd come down. My muddy boots rested against the bench. I rested my elbows on my knees and held the sides of my cheeks in the palms of my hands. I let myself be captivated by the view. Unable to look away from the lake, the mountains, and the patches of glistening snow, I felt someone approach me. I had no fear. While I was aware that someone was walking down the path to the picnic table I was sitting on, I never looked.

The person came around the other side of the table and sat on the top, mimicking my stance, resting their muddy boots on the wooden seat. They placed their elbows on their knees and clasped their hands together with their fingers intertwined.

I never looked over completely; I only glanced out of the corners of my eyes. Their hands were masculine, and even though their boots were dirty, their hands were pristinely clean. We did not speak, but a lot of thoughts raced through my mind. It was as if we were meant to meet here, looking at this surreal view together. I thought to myself, *This is Richard.* I wanted so badly to lean over and rest my head against his shoulder. But I did not.

I heard a thought in my head say, *Yes, it is,* but I realized that the thought was in a different voice than my own. It *was* Richard.

My mind raced. *You wanted it to be this way. You created all of this for me?*

His words came out swiftly and unbearably simple: *Yes, I did.*

Past encounters with Richard in dreams had always been heart-wrenching. They were usually a combination of us crying uncontrollably together, me begging for answers and missing someone who was right there in front of me. They were nightmares. My anguish was usually too powerful for me to sit with him, even in dreams, so I was unable to bask in the closeness I longed for.

This time was different. I wanted to cry, but I did not. I wanted to shake him, or hug him, but I did not. It seemed easy enough to reach over and put my hand on top of his, clasped together, but I did not. This time was to be spent sitting with each other, letting the missing of someone dissipate. His presence for me and my presence for him in this moment had to be enough. I stayed mesmerized by the views he'd created for me to enjoy with him. The scene is etched into my brain as if I had taken a picture of it.

No goodbyes occurred. I woke up and the dream was over. I couldn't help but feel how great Richard's soul was. If he created all of that for me, then his soul had to be at peace.

I lay there in my bed with the morning light creeping in, not wanting to forget a single detail of my dream. I had a gut feeling that what Richard had shown me in the dream, the spectacular views of the lake and the mountain ranges, meant that I would see them again one day. Maybe when my future husband and I were vacationing somewhere new, or in a state park out west. Or maybe when I was very old, gray, and wrinkly, and it was my time. The path I took to the lake could have very well been the path to eternity, and those views felt like Heaven. At least I hoped Heaven would be as beautiful and as filled with nature as my dream.

I knew that someday I would see a picnic table set before a picturesque view with a small, winding, dirt path leading to it. When this happened, I would walk down the path, and when I reached the picnic table, I would sit on the tabletop. Holding my cheeks with my hands, elbows resting on my knees, I would look out to the mountain range and the crystal lake. Next time, I would look over to the other side of the table. Next time, I would see the muddy boot prints on the bench of the picnic table from someone who had been there before. And maybe I would imagine that they were Richard's muddy boot prints; maybe I would somehow be right.

That would make me smile.

CHAPTER 5

Home

F ar too often, the way someone dies can become their whole reputation, especially if there is a stigma attached to it. Especially if it was tragic.

But what happens to those people who miss the *person* they lost and not the title society has given them? What happens to the meaning of the entire life that was lived when you remove the horrific parts from the end? What happens to all of us?

It can take a conscious decision day after day to reclaim what their life truly was. If you do it right, it heals you. If you do it right, it teaches you. But it does take time. None of us want to be remembered based solely on how we leave this world. We want to be remembered for the life we lived in its entirety. I took Richard's identity back from what society knew him as, back from what happened to him. I've reclaimed who he truly was: my brother.

I want to take you back to a long cement-and-gravel driveway, cracked and breaking in pieces because of the cars driving across it over the years, which leads up to a ranch style home. A front door with a glass windowpane in the center opens up to the entrance with brick walls. There is a small dining room to the left, and a coat closet is tucked away in the right corner. A kitchen, laundry room, room over the garage, family room, two bathrooms, and three bedrooms, all pretty ordinary, make up the square footage of this home.

This is the home I grew up in. It is anything but ordinary to me. It is extraordinary. The front door with the window in it was installed after years of my parents saving up for renovations. The brick steps in front of that door are the same, but I look at them and I remember the wooden wheelchair ramp my brother and cousin built when my grandma moved in with us for a year. The brick walls in the entrance that used to be the front porch add character to our home. In the small coat closet, Richard and I put on every jacket on Christmas mornings to find our last gifts during scavenger hunts. I would always scare myself into thinking someone was hiding in the closet when I was home alone as a kid.

I can trace my hand delicately across every surface and tell you a story. The wooden kitchen island that my brother built for our mom when he was in high school still stands, and meals are prepared there every day. The wall in the laundry room is covered in Sharpie archives of our heights and ages that my dad insisted on documenting every year, the last mark for each of us labeled with "Going off to college." I can still remember standing as tall as I could, manifesting the good posture that I never managed to maintain on a daily basis, and then turning around to see if I had caught up to my brother's height. I never did catch up to him, but when I was younger, my eyes would open wide as I glanced further up the wall of tick marks with a fluttering hope that I would get there someday.

Through the bay window in the dining room, I would watch our pine trees bend in the wind during hurricane season, both amazed at their ability to adjust to the conditions around them and terrified that the pressure would be too much and they would give way and crash into our home. If someone had been watching from the outside of that window into our home, they would have seen a lot of my childhood. Meals, conversations, tears, and laughter made up a lot of the memories that played out through that window and around that table.

I remember eating breakfast one Christmas morning, when my brother and I still believed in Santa. We noticed what we thought were reindeer hooves in two perfect lines across our neighbors' roof. My mom went along with the story, and it still might be one of her most clever moments as our mother. She insisted that we were right and let our imaginations wander, while to her, these marks were clearly the frost left over from the cold night starting to melt in spots.

I also remember a food fight with my grandma, my parents, my brother, and myself. It all started with my grandma using her spoon as a catapult and flinging mashed potatoes across the table because she felt like it. Or more likely, one of us had said something smart, but I am going to believe she just wanted to do it. She was a fire-cracker. We all laughed until our stomachs ached; the good kind of ache that can only happen when you love the people around you and aren't afraid to be a fool in front of them.

I remember playing tag with my dogs, weaving in and out of the columns in the entryway and jumping out from behind them. These lead to the family room. So much of my life happened in the family room. Most of our family photographs have our fireplace in the back-ground, from when my mom and I had matching Christmas dresses when I was a toddler to the whole family posing in nice clothes before we went to an important event. Life happened in our family room, and I believe the fireplace is symbolic for the coming together of a family. That was why my family consciously decorated the mantel for holidays, why we chose to display family photographs and mementos there.

The mantel above the fireplace was where we traditionally displayed our stockings during Christmas time. Every year, I would take the stockings one by one out of the boxes we'd pulled from the attic. But one year, this tradition was suddenly different. When I got to the last stocking, the fourth stocking, we all took a moment to quietly sigh, and my sigh was so full of grief that it knocked the air out of me.

Once I left home, my mother decorated for Christmas by herself for the very first time. I can picture her holding the last stocking tightly, hugging it to her chest. She may have sunken into a chair and cried. She likely finally got the courage to hang it up on the nail where it belonged, the nail hammered into the mantel, the nail that had been wedged there for over a decade or longer. Maybe she took a step back and stared at it with thoughts racing through her mind.

The green stocking that she placed there matches my father's green stocking. But on Christmas morning, it remained empty, while the others were stuffed with small presents. Empty because it is my broth-er's stocking, and it will always be my brother's stocking.

CHAPTER 6

Mustangs

My dad never told us much about his childhood, but when he and my brother brought a 1966 teal Mustang home from Greensboro, North Carolina, a few of his memories began to peek through the cracks. He told us that when his dad, my grandfather, would take him to McDonald's, he would open the glove compartment on the passenger side. My dad mimicked the motion in our Mustang, pressing the button to the glove compartment. It popped open, and sure enough, I saw that it created the perfect ledge, essentially a dinner tray, just like he'd described.

Dad pointed to a circle and told me, "This is where my Coke would go," then shifted his hand over to the adjacent indentation and added, "and this is where I'd place my carton of fries."

When the teal Mustang rolled into our driveway, the loose rocks popping and crunching under its tires, the rumbling of the engine announced that Dad and Richard were home. One look at her told me she was special.

Growing up, my brother and dad had baseball and pretty much every other sport to bond over. I played sports when I was younger, but when middle school came along, I never once made it past the second cut during tryouts of any sport I tried out for. I tried golf once but accidentally drove the golf cart into one of the wood columns that held up the carport to the bathrooms between the tenth and eleventh holes. So that was the end of golf for me, which was fine because I found it boring. Come to think of it, I am not quite sure how we ventured into car shows and antique mustangs together after the golf cart accident. My dad probably figured taking me to a place where all of the cars were parked and the keys were not in the ignitions was a safer bet.

I think we were both in search of a hobby that the other also liked. At the same time I started showing interest in cars and car shows, Dad picked up a camera and began showing interest in photography. The two of us casually came together in my teenage years and grew new layers to our bond, layers I would need years later. It's within those layers that I was able to come to him in the night, panicked that Richard's passing was my mind playing tricks on me in those first months after he died. I just couldn't believe that what my head was telling me was right, and Dad helped to steady my breathing as he reluctantly reassured me that this was the reality.

So Richard had baseball and sports to bond with Dad, and as a teenager, I would grow to have cameras, Mustangs, and tires with huge rims. Dad would pick out car shows to attend most weekends, and I began going with him. We would walk around those car shows, hot in the sun and almost melting on the black asphalt, with our cameras in our hands. Dad looked at the engines while I picked the color schemes I liked best. I looked at the exterior paint, and I noticed if there was any rust or cracks in it, squatting down and eyeballing the corners closest to the bumpers and the edges of the doors. If I did not like the colors, if the paint job was cracking in places, or if there was any hint of rust, I just imagined what the underbelly looked like, and I would think that there was probably a better car to photograph down the aisle somewhere.

I learned words like "fastback" and "Shelby." I began to tell the difference from the real Shelbys and the fake ones, the real Saleens and the fake ones. I would blow right past the 1980s models of the Mustang, and my dad always chuckled at my distaste for them. I personally felt that they did not belong at car shows. If you can't tell, they're my least favorite.

There was always a mild rivalry between the Mustang owners and the Corvette owners. Sure, they'd nod and say hello, but they pretty much kept their distance, each feeling that their make of car was better than the other.

It really is funny attending a car show, because all of the cars there are truly built for speed and adventure, the kinds of adventure where you roll down the windows, tossing your hair into the wind, which tousles it into knots—and yet, there was not a speck of dirt on any of these cars. Not one, and I found it comical. The probability that everyone cleaned their cars better than their own homes was almost certain. I liked to think that my dad and I did not fit into that box. We were the cool Mustang owners, even though my dad had a toy car. It was a miniature of his Saleen Mustang, a specially made replica. The mini-Mustang would sit on a mirror turntable on top of the real car's engine, revolving slowly during the entire length of the car show. But we were definitely the cool Mustang owners. Right?

Dad and I would take our Mustang on back roads, listening to nothing, but the engine roaring and the wind whipping together created our own muscle car symphony. They were paved back roads, of course—he was not about to let me drive it down any loose gravel.

The noise of the engine shook the metal of the entire car, even sitting at a stop light. My left foot pressed firmly on the brake pedal, and my right foot instinctively tucked itself under the gas pedal. My ankle flexed upward to lift the gas pedal and relieve the engine for a little while. The rubbery but hard plastic imprinted onto the delicate skin on the top of my foot, but my dad had told me that this helped it from overheating, and we take good care of what is important to us.

That's why when I was alone in my room on the dark, treacherous nights after Richard passed, I knew that when the walls came closing in, I could burst out of my bedroom door and curl up under my dad's arm on the couch. He could not sleep, and maybe he was watching mindless television to escape even for just an hour. But as I would come barging out of my room, a loud and panicked billboard of what he was trying so hard to not think about for a moment, he would curl up with me and rock his adult daughter to steady my breathing. That was something he could do. During this time, he made sure that he would always be there to do what he could by showing up and being there for me.

I do not know what losing an adult child does to a parent. While my parents grieved, they had to wake up every day and help their other adult child navigate the loss of a sibling. I do not know what that does, but I do know that both of my parents held on. They drove their hands down into the mud and remained steadfast. They weathered the hurricane-force winds, like the ones we've grown accustomed to here in Virginia Beach, and they watched their daughter learn to do the same. They could only watch the forecast, not stop the rough weather for me. But as the storm rolled in— always in the late hours of the night—they held tight nonetheless.

That is what matters to me most.

On another one of those brutally hard days, my dad told me to get in the Mustang. We packed up our cameras and went for a drive. Our route offered up a plethora of long roads, few stop lights, and a fifty-five-miles-per-hour speed limit. Then we'd turn around and do it all again toward home.

Before returning home, we pulled the Mustang into the church parking lot across the street from our neighborhood. It was a warm, sunny fall day. Only the smallest hint of the changing weather floated in on the wind. My dad angled the Mustang so it appeared in his viewfinder of his camera with a field of grass behind it, just so, and turned the key, taking it out of the ignition.

We were photographing the exterior when my dad asked me to sit in the driver's seat so he could take my picture. The white-and-teal leather seat squeaked as my jeans pressed into it, and the door popped as I shut it. Dad pressed his shutter button on his camera, verifying his settings with me. After a few tweaks, he took a few more photographs. Then, in the middle of the parking lot, count-less feet away from any plants or flowers, a teal-and-black butterfly fluttered in our direction. As we watched, frozen in time, it made a gradual descent and effortlessly landed on the hood of our teal mustang.

Without a sound, I opened the car door, and miraculously, it refrained from making the popping sound it often did when we got in and out of it. We inched toward the butterfly, and I photographed it, expecting it to fly away just as quickly as it had appeared. But the butterfly stayed with us, lingering, resting on the hood of the car that it matched perfectly.

We stayed there for another half hour and so did the butterfly, all three of us not wanting to go. We refrained from turning on the engine for a long time. We didn't want to leave, because honestly, we both believed that the butterfly was Richard visiting us. We wanted to stay there with the butterfly, with him, and live in this alternate reality, where it was just a normal Saturday and Dad was making a fun memory with his children.

Curiosity got the best of me, as it had been building for thirty minutes, and I wondered if the butterfly was dead. I figured there was no way a butterfly would rest that long on a hot hood of a car. Maybe its wings were singed from the heat of the sun reflecting off of the teal paint. Butterflies' wings flutter almost constantly, and they never stay too long at a flower or on a tree branch.

I approached the butterfly and gently poked it. It jolted up and flapped its teal-and-black wings out in front me as if I'd awoken it from a late afternoon slumber. I instantly regretted my action, wishing the butterfly would land again as it flapped its wings a few more times, gradually coming closer to my face. Then, all at once, it fluttered up, up, up and away from us, ending our fairy tale of an alternate reality, but leaving us with comfort and, most importantly, hope.

CHAPTER 7

Jockey's Ridge

My family was at Jockey's Ridge, watching people try to slide down the hill on their stomachs. Some people actually moved a few feet using this method, but one boy attempting it with a boogie board was another story. The boogie board came to a sudden halt and threw him forward through the air. He actually did seem to travel the farthest, but it was not by sliding. He was airborne and landed several feet away from his boogie board in the hot sand.

I thought, *How do these kids not know how to do this?* Maybe Richard and I had just carried the knowledge from our Mount Trashmore days, when we would roll down the grassy hill at the park just off the interstate in Virginia Beach. We knew to roll down on our sides, hands clasped together and arms shooting out above our heads, legs straight. As we rolled down, we'd pick up speed. On Jockey's Ridge, the kids were likely eating sand and getting it in crevices, where they'd discover it hours later.

Richard and I hiked up the sand dune and proceeded to roll down *correctly*. The other kids quietly watched and learned from us. Soon enough, all of the kids were doing the same thing, nixing their boogie boards altogether.

After our fun, our parents, my brother, and I began to head back down the dunes through the valley of sand to the boardwalk entrance. In the valley, marsh grass had grown where leftover rainwater had settled and created a small ravine. It was the size of a lake, and as I grew more cautious and aware of it, I heard my brother ask to take his shoes off and wade through it the rest of the way to the boardwalk.

I may not have received permission, but after he was twenty

feet ahead of me, I stripped my shoes off and followed him. Sandals in hand, shorts rolled up high, I waded through the water, trailing behind Richard. The water splashed up to my thighs as I navigated the marsh grass. It was clear and glistening, and I could see my toes plunging into the sand, the thought of snakes entering my mind. My arms spread out wide, I could feel my muscles pull from fingertip to fingertip. My right hand closed around my sandals gripping them tight, I attempted to balance myself in the wakeless water.

At that young age, I was already learning from Richard's pull toward nature and exploring. I had always known that he was athletic, especially when it came to baseball. But as I watched him in the distance, settling into the stream and the sawgrass surrounding him, his adventurous side unearthed itself to me for the very first time.

I stopped my childlike desire to catch up to my big brother. I kept my distance and observed him from afar. His posture straightened, and he reached his right hand out to the marsh grass and ran his fingertips along each individual blade as he passed them. Never breaking a piece, he let nature remain the way he'd found it. He was not distracted by the thought of snakes or concerned that he might lose his balance. He felt every grain of sand that his feet sank into and the wake he created in the water. The blades of grass sprang forward with his fingers and then floated effortlessly back to their intended place in the marsh as he let go, never once breaking a blade.

He was free. Free from worry. Free from everything except the creek that had been formed only because of a rainstorm the night before. And as he drifted effortlessly through the ravine, it seemed as if it had been placed here for him alone. Watching my brother on this day, I would later realize, was my first lesson that would teach me about his love for nature.

CHAPTER 8

Graduation

The Outer Banks—where Jockey's Ridge is—was where my most memorable family vacations took place. Our large family began spending every Thanksgiving there. We would all rent a house together in the small town of Corolla.

The barrier islands offered up the perfect quiet getaway for Thanksgiving. There were fewer people in the beach town during the off-season, but the same breathtaking sunsets appeared over the sound. The whole family crammed into one house—cousins, aunts, uncles. It was my favorite way to spend a holiday. Football was always playing on a TV in the background, and my Aunt Neysa would make everyone turn it off when it was time for dinner and played music instead.

She and my Uncle Bobby counted down the minutes until sunset every day. Neysa always draped a shawl over her shoulders, and her curls brushed against the cloth as she smiled and delicately said, "Oh the sunset, the sunset." She and Bobby would stop what they were doing and quietly sneak off to enjoy a glass of wine on the deck together, watching the oranges and reds melt in the sky. Of course, we would all follow suit shortly after them, intruding on their romantic moment, but they'd give us a warm welcome regardless.

When it came time for Richard's college graduation and my high school graduation the same year, my parents proudly gifted us with a week over the summer in the Outer Banks all together. Being peak season, this was a big deal because rates were much higher. We invited friends and family and spent a week in the sun. Neysa and Bobby came down, of course, and we invited other friends and family to spend a few days with us throughout the week.

Another place I loved before I'd ever been there was Big Sky, Montana. It's the complete opposite landscape and terrain of the Outer Banks, but it represented the same qualities for my family. The things we loved about the barrier islands we also loved about the mountain ski town: a week-long trip with the family, quality time spending the entire day outside, and then packing into a condo when we weren't skiing together.

Like the Outer Banks trip after my high school graduation, trips to Big Sky were planned after both of our college graduations. Richard had gone with our dad before and then again with both of our parents. The trip had always fallen on the week that colleges went back to school after winter break, so when I graduated, I would go the following January with them.

My college career was painfully slow, and it took me five and a half years to graduate. At the four-and-a-half-year mark, my brother passed away. Naturally, I had pictured my first Big Sky trip as the four of us. They all loved it there, and from their stories, I knew I would too. I didn't give up on the idea of loving it after Richard passed; in fact, I longed for it that much more. It held a lot of promise; it was a light I could see at the end—or more realistically, in the middle of— the tunnel. Big Sky represented hope for me, and I just knew that it could offer healing if I let it.

A few days before my graduation ceremony, I sat at our dining room table in front of the bay window with some construction paper, paint, and markers, wondering how to decorate my cap. Decorating their cap for the ceremony is everyone's last-ditch effort to show that they're unique. It helps family and friends pick them out from the large crowd all dressed exactly the same. Staring at the blank black canvas of my cap, I had no idea what I wanted to put. I knew more of what I wanted to write on the inside, but still I held it, pondering what I would do. I didn't know how I was going to complete the biggest milestone thus far in my life without my brother there.

Richard's small private college had had an additional ceremony the day before graduation. The graduates were to walk into the church on campus with someone they chose holding their gown, cords, medals, honors, sashes, and caps. During the ceremony, this person gowned and capped the graduate. Richard told me that they were to select someone close to them, someone who meant a lot to them. Then he asked me to be a part of the ceremony with him.

I had proudly held his items and walked beside him as the graduates and their specially selected people walked across the campus in a line to the church. I hadn't realized until that moment that as we became adults, we were growing closer together. Sure, we had been close as children, but now as grown-ups, it was up to us to have a relationship, and we were choosing that. The fact that he chose me meant a lot to me, and as we walked, I thought I would always have my big brother to depend on. We would both always have someone to call. We'd always have someone who knew how important the other was to them.

When it was time to gown the graduates, Richard turned to me and bent his knees slightly so I could reach. I had to stand on my tiptoes to reach up over his head. One by one, I placed the hood, then the sashes, then the cords and medal. I carefully straightened the fabrics and adjusted the cords so the ends were level. Truthfully, I didn't want the moment to end, so I was slow, and Richard probably wondered why.

Making my last adjustments to his capping process, I looked up at him with both hands on one of his sashes. I smiled, flattening the material one more time like a mother would for her son's tie.

I let go, and he smiled at me, then turned to face the front of the church. I turned as well, smiling. I knew to mentally tuck this moment into a special memory folder for myself to hold dear the rest of my life.

I snapped back from my daydream, reminiscing on one of my fondest memories. Still sitting at our table, I looked at all of the graduation tokens in front me, wondering what I should do. I settled in my mind that nothing was going to fill Richard's vacancy. His space would remain empty, but I could try to fill it with sentiment.

I painted a big number thirteen on the top of my cap. Everyone in the crowd would think I'd decorated it for the year I graduated,

2013, but in fact, it was my brother's baseball number. I adhered letter stickers that spelled out "Believe in your dreams." It was cliché but monumental to me at that time in my life because it was a miracle to me that I was graduating. A miracle that I still had dreams, that I had a business already that I was continuously building. It was something I loved. It was going to continue to be my career after graduation. Dreams and a promise of brighter days ahead were the only things that had gotten me there.

I picked up a piece of paper, cut it to fit the inside of the cap, and began writing to Richard. I didn't know what I wanted to write, but I started nonetheless. After I was finished, I taped the note inside, instantly feeling a little relief that I had told him what I felt needed to be said. The elephant in the room was going to be tucked away and placed on the top of my head, but instead of it weighing me down, acknowledging the elephant and giving it a place to go helped me to stand up taller.

After the words were written, I realized that graduating was still going to be hard, but it started to feel possible. I finally felt like I could do it, all of it: walking across the stage, being happy, and celebrating this milestone. Going to Big Sky, healing, and living. The wall that I'd instantly put up after Richard passed seemed to weaken a little, a brick here and there falling out of the wall, and I could see the light starting to shine through.

Days later, I found myself standing in the middle of the arena and walking in a single-file line to the stage. My family and friends spotted me easily with the large "13" on my cap and shouted from the stands. They snapped a picture of me waving and smiling at them. I got to the stage and walked across, shaking hands with the dean and turning the tassel on my cap from one side to the other.

I'd done it! I made my way through the aisles back to my seat. After all the graduates did the same, they announced us as the graduating class of December 2013. Everyone cried out a cheer, and caps started flying into the air. I fell quiet compared to the rest of the graduates, watching the black caps dancing without rhythm in the air.

I took mine off and threw it delicately above me. The cap sailed only a couple feet from my hand before it drifted back down and I caught it. Both relieved that I hadn't lost the cap and elated that I'd participated in the celebratory toss, I put the cap, my letter to Richard, and his baseball number safely back on my head. I was now a college graduate with a degree, and a few weeks later, I would be getting on a plane to Big Sky, Montana.

CHAPTER 9

Big Sky

Only a few weeks after graduating college, I headed to the airport with my parents to travel to Big Sky, Montana. The mountain ski town that I had never been to meant so much more than a family ski vacation to me. I was visiting a place my brother had loved. I was spending a week skiing where he'd snowboarded. I was breathing the air that he had, and if I was lucky, I would unknowingly sit on a ski lift chair that he'd sat on years prior. I was going to try a bison burger, eat dinner in a yurt, and snowmobile in Yellowstone. All of the things that he had done on previous trips, I was finally going to do, and I hoped that Richard would be there with me ... somehow.

Being a photographer, I had this odd urge to take pictures around our home or in nature and search every pixel of them to see if there was a "sign" from Richard. I knew it wasn't likely, but I looked for him in reflections. I looked for signs of him through orbs of light. Behind trees or in the shapes of clouds, I desperately looked for him in my photographs. I've never told anyone that, mainly because it's strange. But to me, grief is the absolute strangest thing in the world. It affects every aspect of you and your life. It can be good and bad in the sense that it can either make you carry a huge weight of sadness or it can inspire you to live life to the fullest and do more of what you love in honor of that person. The strangest part about grief is that it can do both at the exact same time. These opposites can coexist, and we do our best to work through it. I learned early on that there was no way around my grief; I could only go straight through.

To write this accurately in honor of my brother, I have to go straight through all the mess. There are parts of me that don't want to endure the grief, but if I didn't, I would not be writing what I thought made our family and now, more accurately, what truly makes our family. I would not be getting to the depth of why these experiences greatly changed me. The mess of the pain, the grief, the abrupt life change dissipates over time. Just like oil and vinegar, if life gets shaken, it will blend in a colorful mess for a time. But eventually oil and vinegar will separate. Over time, I have learned to separate the pain and grief from my happy and joyous life. But I can sense it there. They will always touch.

I know that this grief has also made me a better person. It fuels some of my decisions, like why I hike and why I spend time in nature.

Big Sky, Montana, is what started all of that for me. It began to mend me in parts of my life that I hadn't realized needed to be healed through the fog of my grief. Big Sky ripped my heart open and then allowed me to piece it all back together again. I believe with the purest depths of my soul that Richard was there to help me put the pieces back together. Just like searching in photographs, I went to Big Sky in search of Richard's presence. I went in search of peace, and that is where I first created the path I wanted for my life. It was the first trail marker of so many to come. Big Sky is where I began to heal.

We traveled with a group from my dad's ski shop. Yes, a beach town ski shop. A wing of his retail store was catered toward trips for other skiers. His business traveled to resorts like Wintergreen in Virginia and Snowshoe in West Virginia for eastern trips. But for each ski season, he would plan a few western trips for his customers. He organized their lodging, lift tickets, and flights, as well as some itinerary options. The group included my parents and myself, some longtime friends of the shop—like John, who my family knew long before I was born—and other customers. My dad organized these trips every year to different resorts, but Big Sky was one they went to every year. That year had even more meaning because the three of us had a secret. We were going to spread some of Richard's ashes during our trip.

The un-poetic part about this was when my dad looked up TSA rules for flying with ashes, first to make sure it was legal, and second to see how he needed to do it so the TSA would not question him in front of all of his customers. He did not want to have to explain that his son was in his carry-on ski boot bag. There are logistics to these kinds of things, and my dad understandably did not want to make a scene.

He also did not want to have any chance of losing the ashes, so he placed them in a Zip-Loc baggie inside his ski boot bag and took that as his carry-on. On smaller planes, there seems to always be a flight attendant standing right before you get on the plane, taking the carry-ons that they deem too large for the compartments in the plane. They will politely ask you to volunteer your bag to be checked and assure you that you can pick it up right at an entrance just like this one at your destination. They will reach for your bag with the claim tag in their hand before you have time to agree or disagree. In an instant, your bag is checked and rolling down the conveyor belt outside to be loaded in the bottom of the plane.

As luck would have it, as our line inched toward the plane, we noticed a flight attendant selecting luggage from the people ahead of us.

I always get anxious at that moment, because usually when I travel, my camera equipment is in my carry-on. I always imagine myself getting very stern and forbidding them to take my luggage. I clutch the most expensive items I own. I act "holier than thou"— again, only in my head—and become a stubborn toddler.

But this time, it was different. This was my brother.

Even though I'd been known to clutch my carry-on like a child, I had never seen someone try to hide a blatantly oversized boot bag with their body. That's exactly what Dad did while we approached the flight attendant. This would have been comical to watch if I hadn't been aware of why my dad was attempting to shield his obtrusive boot bag. He could not bear the thought of his son being in the bottom of the plane, tossed around like any other piece of luggage. I could not bear that thought either.

The flight attendant spotted our huge bag and began to reach for it, red tag in hand with the rubber band stretched out around her fingertips, ready to mark the boot bag. I pushed forward, volunteering to check my luggage in its place. She reluctantly agreed; she was clearly right about my dad's bag being oversized.

The bag did not fit underneath the seat in front of me, and it did not fit in the above compartments. I was the weak link with the shortest legs, so the boot bag went under my feet. But I got to fly to Montana with Richard's ashes safe and sound in my sitting area on the plane rather than being tossed around with the luggage beneath us. I was grateful, even if my knees were almost at my chest. As I glanced around at all of the passengers that did not know our heartbreaking secret, an odd feeling came over me. For a moment, I was relieved and happy because Richard was making it to Big Sky with us.

I will admit, Big Sky held a lot of meaning to me without my having been there before. As I sat on the plane and watched the sun rise over the mountains of Montana, I expected a lot from this place. That was probably unfair of me, but I also had the feeling that it could deliver. I gazed out the window and daydreamed about all of the promises Big Sky held for me.

We landed at the small airport in Bozeman, a town in a valley with snow-capped mountains surrounding it. I searched for my ski jacket, because I'd flown in from mild weather to an area that was already covered in snow. But, unlike where I am from, where the city shuts down with an inch of snow, this town thrived in their winter wonderland. A large bus took our entire group from the airport to Big Sky Resort. At first, I was apprehensive about the mountain roads with the large bus trudging along. The roads were plowed but not clear, the snow seemed to be packed down, and our bus was wide and bulky. There would have been a twenty-car pileup at every turn if it had been my hometown, which made me a little uneasy. But soon enough, views of mountains, elk, deer, and a river alongside the road engulfed my attention span.

I sat next to John, who I knew from my dad's ski shop. I always remembered John as a fun, vivacious man with a ponytail. Later in life, I enjoyed talking with him and listening to his stories more and more. At the time of the trip, John was sans ponytail, but he was wearing a big cowboy hat and cowboy boots. I was used to seeing him in the boots at the ski shop, but the cowboy hat was new to me. He and I had a mutual love for photography. While I photographed people and weddings, he and his wife loved to photograph nature, scenery, and animals. That's why I sat next to him on the bus: because the entire forty-five-minute ride to the ski resort, John pointed out every bald eagle to me. He was like a bald eagle wizard. You would have thought they were being summoned just for him. He would point each perching eagle out, just as excited for one as he was for the next.

Those bald eagle sightings were still in the valley. Before long, the mountains seemed to grow straight into the air, halting only for a small river stream where humans came along and built a skinny road to follow it. John told me that we could see more bald eagles along the winding river because they would be in those trees to spot fish and other small animals. Sure enough, as John finished his sentence, we saw a bald eagle gliding just above the river's surface, its wings spread out over the winding and rushing water, wingtips grazing the surface. This eagle glided effortlessly above the water, following the twists and turns of the river. It flew like this in our sights for only a short distance, but I felt as if I was seeing him in slow motion. John and I fell silent, both of us mesmerized while gazing at the eagle.

As quickly as the moment came, it passed us by. John and I looked at each other in silence and smiled. He gave me a tight squeeze around my shoulder, then went back to pointing out elk and talking about the big horn sheep peppered along the mountainside. Seeing the bald eagles and other animals was outstanding. I was overjoyed to be there. But seeing that one particular bald eagle gliding above the river within an hour of being in Montana stunned me. Gazing out the window, I imagined how the week could possibly get any better—and I was still just sitting on the bus! It turned out that that experience was only the beginning.

During the week we were there, every morning we'd get up before sunrise for the largest breakfast buffet I have ever seen, the kind where you overindulge yourself with coffee, waffles, fruit, sausage, and gravy. You give yourself the works on your overflowing plate. They also had eggs and an omelet bar, but I'm not a huge fan of eggs.

I sipped on my coffee at a round table with my parents and a few other people. We watched the snowcats as they finished grooming the ski slopes just outside the floor-to-ceiling windows. At this point, I could only see the moon in the sky and the headlights from the snowcats. As I drank my piping hot coffee, I watched the light gradually get brighter and brighter on the mountain, illuminating the trees, the details of the snowcats, and the corduroy lining they created on the slopes. The sun rose on the other side of the building, so we didn't see the sunrise, but with each passing minute, the mountain range revealed more of itself in all its glory. Lone Peak began to peek through the early morning light (pun intended!). It was a magnificent show every morning just for us.

The previous owner of my dad's ski shop, Nick, had originally introduced our ski family to Big Sky. It was his favorite place. I remember watching his home ski videos and a particular one of him recording Lone Peak at a breakfast while watching the sun gradually light her up. As the video started, Nick was not in the frame. Even though it was quiet, almost perfectly still, I could sense him there by the slight shake of the camera. Once I could see the peak from the rising sun, Nick said in an almost whisper, "There she is. Isn't she beautiful?"

I thought of this clearly rhetorical question as I brought my coffee cup to my lips that morning. I took a sip and then gradually lifted my mug out in front of me and toasted to the mountain, to Nick, and to Richard. I whispered to them, "She is."

We always dressed from head to toe in our ski gear and were ready for the ski lifts right at opening time. Big Sky usually didn't have lines at their lifts, but if they had, we would have always been the first group in line. We started each morning with one trail together called "Mr. K." I loved this trail because it was a long ski lift ride high up the mountain, but I realized that I was nowhere close to the summit once I glided off the lift.

We traversed down a narrow bend with an amazing view of "the Bowl" way out in front of us. The Bowl was a wide mountain basin whose slopes looked as if they had been carved from the sides of a cereal bowl with a spoon. It was mostly devoid of trees, allowing skiers and snowboarders to make sweeping S-turns down the mountain face. Do not let that description fool you though; "devoid of trees" means there was nothing to anchor my eyesight too. It means I could see nothing but stark white terrain with no dimension. It means very high elevation, and the only way down is through the sea of white. It could make you throw up your bowl of cereal from that morning if you aren't prepared.

Along the bend to my left was the mountain range, and on my right was a tiny burrito hut with a small deck around it to take in the views and eat lunch. Next to the hut were signs marking a "no drop-in zone" for skiers down the mountainside. Because of this, I always tried to hug the left side. The bowl carved perfectly into the mountain way out in front of us, and we crossed the bottom of it to pick up Mr. K. The slope was smooth and wide. I have yet to find a more perfect trail to get my ski day started. After our first run together, we split off into smaller groups and ski trails. Then we met back up in time for lunch in the cafeteria.

Later in the week, during the afternoon, we decided to do our last run before heading to the village for lunch. One superstition we believe is that you are never supposed to mention it being your last run of the day ... ever. I had not yet been on the trail that the group picked, but the group had taken me on some runs that were harder than I was used to, and I'd done fine on those. I figured this trail would not be any different. Someone at Big Sky had decided to name the trail "Ambush," so thank you to whoever that was.

We skied down another flat catwalk on the other side of the resort to get to the Ambush trail, and while I skied past slopes peeling off to my left, I was thankful that each one was not Ambush. When we approached the next one, I leaned to the right, hoping everyone else would do the same, but a few people in our group peeled off to the left and dropped in. Their heads disappeared, and I reluctantly turned to the left of the catwalk and peered down, edging my skis forward slowly. "This is Ambush? You have got to be kidding me," I said under my breath. Letting out a loud sigh, I prepared to drop in. The tips of my skis just peeking over the edge, I turned in, now completely committed.

Ambush was steep, but it wasn't completely wide open. Making my turns through the groomed snow, I was comforted by the few trees in the center of the trail, helping me to anchor to something in the vast white area. After I skied past the small patch I was using as an anchor, the blanket of white took over, and nothing but white terrain filled the wide and steep slope down the rest of the mountain. I began to panic.

I had been skiing well all week, so my dad didn't think to stay close by. He skied almost eighty percent of the way down without worrying about me. When he finally turned and looked up at me, he might as well have been miles away, sitting in the cafeteria, blowing on his hot chili to cool it down, feet kicked up by a roaring fire.

My body was frozen, but my mind ran wild. Dad couldn't do anything, nor could he tell what was going on. He looked like an ant to me, and I became lightheaded as the line of trees on either side of the slope spread out farther and farther away from me. I blinked and continued to stare at them. John had told me to do this on another steep slope just the day before, to try to ground myself again instead of looking down the mountain. The trees continued to stretch farther, and I stayed off-kilter no matter how many times I blinked. My cheeks warmed, melting the snowflakes instantly as they touched my skin. I took my glove off to dab my cheek dry, and I realized that my face was sopping wet from my own warm tears. I'd been crying for a while. My eyes blurry from tears, a part of me thought that I would never escape from this slope on the mountain. I had so much more to go; how could I possibly get there?

Anxiety ambushed me. Fear ambushed me. Panic ambushed me. Sadness ambushed me as well. I quickly realized that my anxiety, fear, and panic were not just about the Ambush trail itself, but also about my life ambushing me. Richard passing away, our family being heart-broken, and all of the turmoil we'd lived with for years was coming to a head. It all ambushed me, and I became paralyzed in my own self-doubt and sorrow.

Still, I had a choice: I could have stay paralyzed and defeated. I could have curled up into a ball. I could have let the skiers above trample over me when they came flying down and didn't see me laying there—or, I could buck up and get off the mountain. I could cry, I could be afraid and anxious, but I also had the choice to buck up. I could have moments of both. I could sit in the feeling and then make a choice.

Through this newfound determination and my blurry tears, I dug my ski pole into the snow and pushed off, making a quick, sharp turn to my side. I repeated each turn over and over again, making zig-zagging lines in the snow, digging my edges in. It looked like a jackhammer had been there; I could sense it, but I didn't dare look behind me to see for myself. I did all of this through a constant flow of tears, my legs shaking, and occasionally blurting curse words. Among the curses, I also let out a few pleas. I cried out to myself, to God, to Richard, "Please help me off this mountain. Please keep me safe. Please help me." I repeated these pleas, some out loud and some in my mind—some for my present situation and some for my future— over and over again through my sharp and ungraceful turns. And I realized that that's the thing about bucking up: it isn't always graceful.

Eventually, I lifted my head and realized I was most of the way down the slope, which was flattening out under my skis. My ankles no longer felt like they were breaking, and the edges of my skis no longer dug into the snow on one side. They relaxed, and I relaxed.

I skied past my dad, still having my adult version of a temper tantrum through the snow. And as I drifted by, overwhelmed and pissed off, he called out, "What happened?" I ignored him. I could hear his skis gliding in the snow behind me as he followed me down a small hill to the village. He could tell that I needed space, but he had no clue why. I was deep in my own mind and shaken to my core when my dad called out again behind me, "Do you hear that music? Do you hear what song is playing?"

I shook my head vigorously to clear out my thoughts so I could listen. As we approached the village, the outside speakers sang a familiar tune: *"But you better get your face on board the very next train*

*… Evil woman … Evil woman … Evil woman (you're an evil woman),
evil woman."* Electric Light Orchestra sang out through the speakers.

Smiling, I slowly glanced over my shoulder at my dad, who was
smiling too. The tension from Ambush melted away from me. My
dad and brother used to play this song for me when I was grumpy
as a child or throwing a tantrum. Chasing me around the house,
they would belt out this tune. I acted like I absolutely hated it, but
secretly I loved all three-plus minutes of the song. I would jump over
couches or cut corners through the living room and hallways to run
away from them. If I hid behind a couch, they would jump onto that
couch and lean over the back of it, singing this song and reaching
their arms out trying to grab me. "Evil Woman" by Electric Light
Orchestra is a song that my brother and dad used as a way to say,
"Relax, calm down; it's going to be okay."

There in the village, it made me laugh, but I also desperately
wanted to cry again. Dad was still smiling, but his eyes changed as
he studied mine. A layer of water filled his eyes, and I knew that
without words, he realized what had happened to me on that mountain. While tears filled in the corners of our eyes, I said, "Richard
made it to Big Sky with us after all." We clicked our boots out of our
bindings, and Dad draped his arm around my shoulders and leaned
over to say, "I know. Let's go get some chili."

After lunch, we skied a few more trails. I convinced myself that
I could not end the ski day with Ambush, so I stuck to Mr. K and
other wonderful green trails. When we finally headed in for the day,
we were extra careful not to mention at the start of the trail that it
would be our last one for the day. Once inside our condo, I quickly
changed and grabbed my headphones, a book, and my journal, and
headed down to one of the two large stone fireplaces in the lodge.

I did this often while my parents headed to the heated outside
pool. I loved to sit at the large stone fireplace and write and think
about the day I'd just had skiing where my brother once had snowboarded. The larger of the two fireplaces was made from intricate but
imperfect stone from floor to ceiling. As the fire crackled and warmed
the room, I looked over every stone. On either side of the fireplace

stood tall stacks of chopped wood. A man came up every so often to throw more wood on the fire, making some of the embers float up the fireplace as he messily rearranged the blocks of wood.

Picturing myself nestling into one of the cozy chairs, resting my sore knees and calves in front of the large fireplace, I came around the corner to find no empty seats available. Reluctantly, I walked to the other side of the lodge to the smaller, cozier stone fireplace. I overlooked this one often because the other one was so grand. With no one else there, I settled into the couch directly in front of the hearth and placed my feet on the ledge of the coffee table. I opened my book and thumbed through its pages to where I'd previously left off. Oddly enough, or perhaps not oddly at all, the book I'd chosen to bring on that trip was a story about a woman who began to hike to reclaim her life after loss and other tribulations.

The stones making up the fireplace were separated by two bulging logs, each the length and width of two separate trees. I imagined that they cut down two trees just outside and carried them into the lobby when they were constructing the lodge, ready to make the design of this fireplace come to life. They were sanded down and glossed over with some sort of a finish. The center of the logs that lined up with the opening to the fireplace were charred a darker brown, almost black, from the smoke and ash from the fire over the years. They were clearly old and worn, but to me, that gave them character. They had stories within their grains.

Thumbing through the pages of my book and reading the author's words quickly made my mind wander to my own thoughts. I'd always dabbled with writing. When my grandmother passed away, I wrote journals and journals of poems that I later cringed at. It was typical middle school anguish and despair, the kind that makes people feel foolish as an adult for ever feeling that way. Later in college, I wrote a lot about our life in those past few years, and the turmoil my family had been going through still. But I always wrote about the hope I held onto. The hope I had for my brother. My adult self—well, my college-aged adult self—did not want any part of the middle school anguish and resentment when it came to writing. Later I backed off because I was not sure what direction I wanted my writing to go in. Once most of the fog of my grief lifted, I was not sure how I wanted to tell our story. I was not sure how to adequately remember Richard. I was afraid to open it all up to the world. But nonetheless, the calling to write came back to me even when I tried to leave it.

What are my words going to be? Do I have the right words to begin with? I always silently asked myself when sitting down to put pen to paper. A familiar tune started to hum through my earbuds. The upbeat, instrumental music built for nearly a minute before a word was ever sung. "Life in Technicolor II" by Coldplay played in my headphones while chills traveled up my spine. My chills danced in a revolving pattern, traveling up and out through my ears into the earbuds and back up my spine to repeat the pattern. The song continued, "*Time came a-creeping. . . . Oh and time's a loaded gun ... (every road is a ray of light) ... It goes on. . . . Time only can lead you on, still it's ... such a beautiful night. . . . Gravity, release me ... and don't ever hold me down. . . . Now my feet won't touch the ground.*" My eyes began to water. It was one of the songs that had played at Richard's memorial service.

When the second half of the four-minute song chimed in, I looked up from the pages I was reading and straight ahead into the stone hearth. Through the orange flames, a grate was holding up the firewood from the bottom of the fireplace. On both ends of the wrought iron grate, the iron curved, turning into two butterfly shapes.

"Butterflies?" I questioned.

In the middle of a winter wonderland, inside a ski lodge that was heavily decorated in bear statues and wood carvings, someone had come along and said, "Hey, let's get a butterfly steel grate for the fireplace."

It doesn't really matter why this choice was made; someone made the choice, and there they were before me as the fire turned them into beautiful silhouettes. I watched them as the flames swayed, creating an optical illusion that the butterflies were fluttering their wings, almost dancing.

I could not tell how many more minutes were left of that song, or how many tears fell as I silently and motionlessly stared past the flames and the butterflies. Thinking about the entire day and all of Richard's signs overwhelmed me. I watched the embers break away from the wood logs; floating, they mimicked the flutter of a butterfly's wing. The iron butterflies kept me company while I rested in front of the fireplace; never rushing me, they danced with the flames, while I pondered what it all meant.

CHAPTER 10

Snow Duck

I remember a particular snow day, more through looking at pictures than from my own memory. One year, when Richard and I were very young, during one of the maybe two proper snowfalls that Virginia Beach receives a year, the snow came and blanketed our front yard in white for a few days. We have home movies of us playing in the front yard, making a snowman and throwing snowballs at each other. We walked in slow, robotic movements in our thick layers, attempting to reach the ground to form our snowballs in our mittens, all the while laughing. We never had snowballs made at the same exact time, so when someone would throw one into the other's face, a tantrum would occur. The victim would storm off with the slowest angry walk you would ever see, snow pants crunching with every step, breaking the silence that our numb and wet faces wanted.

The tantrums were too comical for us to be able to stay mad for long. Snow days did not happen often where we lived, so we let bygones be bygones and continued the slow-motion snowball battle.

When I was younger, I was either as sweet as can be or a true terror. We have proof of this, and family members never let me forget it. My Aunt Neysa nicknamed me "Baby B," and I'll let you figure out what the B stood for. My dad nicknamed me "Princ-ass"—lovingly, of course! I always secretly loved the "Princ-ass" nickname. And the original owner of Dad's ski shop nicknamed me "Little Terror." It was universally understood that I was … moody.

Like I said, there is a lot of proof to back up these nicknames. We have a family video of us throwing snowballs at each other, laughing and moving slowly in our puffy snow clothes, and then one snowball hits me square in the face. In the video, I stormed off, screaming, knees hitting my chest and my arms swinging back and forth. When I would storm off as a child, I meant it, and I always made it known that this was my "storming off walk." Combined with the thick layers of clothing and wading through the snow, this walk was … truly special.

There's another home video that shows me going to hug my grandma on Christmas morning, and my foot stepped directly into her piping hot coffee, which she had placed on the ground beside her to receive my hug. That storming off walk could have won an Emmy for most dramatic actress.

In the video at hand, however, the day was salvaged because we made a snow duck instead of a snowman. I instantaneously transformed back to my sweet side and made the snow duck with my brother and my parents.

With help from our dad, we packed and rolled snowballs on the ground to create the body, and our mom was there to photograph it all. It was clear that he was a snow duck and not a snowman in the picture: the individual snowballs morphed into one for his body, with a triangular head instead of a picturesque circular one for a snowman. We dotted the eyes with rocks.

Dad belly laughed and widened his eyes when he thought of a good idea, the kind of idea that he instantly knew would make a lasting memory for us. He ran inside with us running after him, chasing one another to the kitchen. Dad chuckled as he took out a slice of leftover pizza from the fridge. "This is going to be awesome," he exclaimed. His idea was to use the slice of pizza for the mouth. When he told us what he was thinking, Richard jumped up and down, laughing with Dad, and I smiled up at both of them, letting out a childish laugh alongside my brother.

Back outside, Dad handed the cold pizza slice, thick with a solid block of cheese, to my brother, letting him do the honors. He created a groove in the snow duck's head under its rocks for eyes and motioned for my brother to place the slice in the groove. Richard's wide grin surfaced as he placed the pizza. The snow duck was born on a day forever etched into our minds as one of the best snow days of our lives.

We wrote out "Snow Duck" with a thick red arrow on a piece of paper, which we adhered to a piece of wood. Richard placed the sign in the snow at the foot of the snow duck, to give our neighbors passing by an explanation of our creation.

My mom ushered us next to our snow duck and clicked the shutter button on her camera. In taking that picture, she froze that snow day in time for us.

CHAPTER 11

Move Mountains

There is a photograph of Richard that has moved mountains. It has reached coastlines across the U.S. It has been the headline photograph on the front page of *The New York Times*. It's the photograph that distraught and sometimes grieving parents first see when they search words like "Adderall addiction." I never thought his name would be so closely associated with terms like this that a computer algorithm would pull up his picture in less than a tenth of a second. Unfortunately, thanks to technology, they are forever linked together.

This photograph of Richard first sat in a frame on an easel in the front of a church. I stood next to it as I spoke to our family and his friends. It became the face I pictured when I thought about Richard, when I talked to him, when I wanted to remember him as being happy. Before this photograph became associated with any of this tragedy, it was simply a photograph of Richard, wide-eyed and smiling. He had a baby blue button-down shirt on, and his deeply rich brown eyes glistened with the flash from the camera.

And before that, it was a moment in time—a celebratory time— when I walked up to Richard for a photo. He was taking a break from dancing at our cousin's wedding, sitting with his arms folded on the back of a chair. As the music thrummed through the DJ's speakers, I motioned to Richard, asking him to smile as I pressed my shutter button. I did not know then what this photograph would become. I did not know what it would represent.

His eye contact when I look at him in this photograph is powerful. Richard's life was powerful, and losing him was powerful. I remember walking up to the stage and standing next to his photograph to speak to everyone at his memorial service. But really, what I had written to say that day was only for him. I wore a light purple sweater and a floral purple-and-green scarf, my favorite scarf. I never wore that outfit again after that day.

Frankly, losing Richard altered the course of my life no matter how I look at it, and when I want to imagine Richard as more powerful than what happened to him, I think of this same photograph every time.

Years after he passed, I was hiking at Overall Run, quite cold and drenched from continuous rain. Weighed down by my soaked-through black fleece vest, I was trying to keep up the pace. Nine other women were hiking with me, and the incline to the frozen waterfall was affecting me more than usual. My heart felt like it was beating out of my chest, a feeling all too familiar, instantly reminding me of how I had felt when I found out Richard had passed away. My heart pulsated through my ears, and I started to believe that it might actually jump out. I knew the summit was close. I focused on getting to sit and refuel with the peanut butter sandwich I had packed in my backpack.

When we got to the summit, I photographed the frozen waterfall and the clouds rolling in from the distance over the mountains. Then I photographed each woman with the waterfall behind them. When I pulled my sandwich out, I found that it had been smashed in its bag by my water bottles. But I was too hungry to have any embarrassment as I scooped out the peanut butter stuck against the inside of the plastic bag with my fingers. When I found a big enough piece of bread still intact, I continued scraping out the peanut butter with it. When I was halfway through eating my "sandwich," the rain began again. Everyone started packing up, and I joined in, taking off my fleece vest, replacing it with my extra rain jacket, and storing what was left of my sandwich for later.

I saw the trail sign that indicated the summit was three miles into the whole hike. By the fifth mile, we turned onto a new trail called Ridge Trail. According to the maps I'd read online earlier in the week, this turn was the farthest point from the trail head entrance along the loop we were hiking.

Without warning, my head drifted, feeling light and heavy at the exact same time. I felt as if the back of my neck was being pushed down by intensifying gravity while my forehead was being lifted to float into the sky. I immediately reached for my water, which was strapped to the side of my pack, to try to calm myself down. I didn't tell the other women how I was feeling, because as the hike leader, I was embarrassed to let them know that I was struggling, that I was lightheaded.

Grasping for something, anything to root me to the trail, I pictured that photograph of Richard. Then I began talking to him in my mind. It started to make me feel better, calmer. I kept thinking to him that I could not faint there; we had been through enough hard things, he and I. I told him that I'd dealt with and overcome much harder times, and I was not going to let this be part of my story, or part of this day, at the very least.

Talking to Richard helped, but I quickly realized that my feeling was more than a dizzy spell; it was also anxiety, and it was amplifying. I worried about the possibility that these women would have to carry me out of the trail, and other worst-case scenarios started racing through my mind. I thought to Richard, telling him that I needed more help, more guidance. Without realizing it at first, and I am convinced with Richard's help, I began praying to God.

I prayed for the knowledge that this was anxiety and nothing more. Prayed for God or Richard to give me the strength to complete the hike. Prayed to them, asking for help in that moment, for help making my anxiety dissipate. It helped to calm me, but my body still felt weak. With every flutter of dizziness, I took a gulp of water, and the act of adding the water to my own body weighed me down to the ground a little more with every sip. I reassured myself that I hadn't eaten enough. I told God that although talking to him was foreign to me, it was helping, and I was going to keep talking to him just in case it was the very thing that was soothing me. This was the first time since losing Richard that I had prayed.

I imagined Richard walking just behind me, nudging me toward this moment of surrender and speaking to God. I felt like my body was breaking, like it was failing me. I was in pure panic, edging closer and closer to being so uncomfortable that I thought I might crawl out of my own skin. Once I was in the moment of fear and despair, Richard helped me through it. Once I was through the moment, I learned that I would never have been stranded by God when it truly mattered. When it counted.

This is how God shows up for me now, and although I did feel stranded physically by Him for a long time, it took just as long to realize that spiritually, I wasn't. Spiritually, I will never be alone, because of God and because of Richard. I felt far away from both of them for a long time, but they also led me back to each other over the next several years.

Thinking about both of them, the dizzy spells became only memories, but I kept this picture of Richard in my mind for the rest of the hike. It helped me stay present as I hiked through the rainstorm and the mud on the trail back to our cars. I prayed. I thought. I hiked. I envisioned. I made it.

Two days later, I was home, dry, hydrated, and fed when my mother called me in tears. The same panic set in as my mind wondered, *What happened and to whom?* Mom explained through sobs that she had just ended a phone conversation with a distraught mother, who told Mom that as she lay awake feeling helpless in the night, she had begun to search for ways to help her own son. A bold headline had appeared with a photograph of a man in a baby blue button-down shirt, deeply rich brown eyes, arms folded on the back of a chair, and a captivating smile.

The woman had clicked on this photograph, stunned by the similarities as she read the words from *The New York Times* article. On the phone with my mother, she admitted that in those late hours, she kept clicking her mouse back to the photograph, repeating out loud over and over again, "Richard, please help me save my son's life. Richard, please help me save my son's life," in the dark of her room, the only light in her world shining from the computer screen. The screen captured the light from Richard's eyes, his smile, and his warm skin from the summer sun. In her darkest night, he was her light. That is when she had vowed to find a way to reach out to my mom.

A photograph can be powerful. Richard's life was powerful, and losing him was powerful. Richard moved mountains for me as I pictured him in that memory; his face brought me through to the light. I hope that Richard moved mountains to save this mother's son too.

CHAPTER 12

Butterflies

C ory and I had been dating only eight months when we decided to drive out to the mountains for our first hiking and camping trip together. I was thrilled that I'd found someone who valued hiking and the mountains as much as I did. The windows were all rolled down, and as we drove over the hills with farmland on both sides zipping by, I looked at him in the driver's seat and thought to myself that this was exactly what I wanted; he was what I'd been looking for.

We eventually arrived at Peaks of Otter in Bedford, Virginia. Before setting up camp, we decided to start the hikes nearby. We decided to do two hikes but start with the lesser-known trail there, the Harkening Hill Loop Trail, described as 3.3 miles of woodland trail opening up to distant views. We began our trek, which marked our very first hike together.

I began to wonder where the trail was going to open up. As we hiked, it seemed that it would only ever be covered with dense vegetation overgrown onto the path. I constantly thought about ticks while the brush grazed my bare ankles. Poison ivy came to mind as well, and I made sure to keep my hands up to avoid touching the overgrowth. The problem was that Cory had the backpack, so I had nowhere to put my hands. I was hiking in front of him with my arms bent and my hands in the air. I knew I must have looked a little prissy, attempting to avoid touching the mysterious plants. But truly I was just trying to avoid poison ivy and ticks.

Without any hint to us that the scene was changing, sunlight appeared on my hands. Gradually the shadows of the trees crept up my arms to my shoulders, and then my skin warmed entirely from the sun. I looked up from watching my every step to avoid poison ivy and saw wildflowers as tall as my chest surrounding us. A skinny dirt path was the only thing that prevented us from being engulfed into the field, and I was in awe as my eyes traveled from flower to flower. My mind went from worrying about ticks to running my fingers through the wildflowers on both sides of me. My open palms touched the tops of the flowers like I was skimming over a calm surface, waist-deep in a lake. I did not notice anything else at first, but then a fluttering movement caught my attention in the corner of my eye. I adjusted my focus and finally saw them: butterflies fluttering through the rows and rows of stems from wildflower to wildflower, their wings painted with browns and yellows flying all around us.

When my eyes began to water, I allowed them to fill without reservation. I happily laughed out loud; I had a lot to tell Cory about butterflies. Of course, I had shared part of Richard's story with him, but I still had a lot to tell him about Richard and my grief.

Flashbacks of so many other butterfly encounters danced through my mind. The teal-and-black one that landed on our teal mustang. The ones that followed me for a while as I ran trails back home. Soon after my brother passed away, butterflies became my sign from him. One time, Richard had told me to grab my camera and head to the backyard with him, swinging the back door open. The memory came flooding back to me as I stood in that field. "Ryan! Bring your camera! I want to show you something. Quick! Come on!" Richard had exclaimed, running out into the sunlight patches on the grass, as the storm door swung shut behind him.

I had done what I was told, interested in the mere fact that he was speaking to me. I went outside and walked up beside him. "Look, Ryan, look!" Richard pointed to the shrubbery near his feet as he bent over to get closer, and there it was: a black and white striped butterfly fluttering about, putting on a show for us.

"Doesn't this look like zebra stripes? Isn't that the mascot of your sorority? Anyway, I thought you would like to photograph it. Hurry, before it flies away!" Richard usually spoke quickly, with minimal pauses between his sentences.

That was the most he had spoken to me in months. He was absent most of the time, even when he was present. *He knows my sorority's mascot? He thinks I would like to photograph this butterfly? He knows I love photography?* I hadn't even been sure that he still thought about me at all. As I quickly snapped a few photographs, a sliver of a smile had appeared on Richard's face, and then our moment was over. I missed his ear-to-ear smile, but I gladly accepted a small one that day.

Bringing me back to the wildflower field and out of my daydream, a larger butterfly floated past me effortlessly. I looked up to the sky as it fluttered by quickly. It looked different from the other, smaller butterflies, so I turned around to see it again. Cory was there, smiling. He told me that the butterfly was black and a teal sort of blue, but he didn't know where it had gone. It seemed to be the only different butterfly in the entire field, similar to the one that landed on my teal '66 Mustang the first fall after Richard was gone.

I asked Cory to help me look around for the butterfly, and he happily agreed. We looked all around the field, carefully standing in our same spots, just turning our heads. Our hands spread out just above the meadow's grass, gracefully grazing its edges in our attempts to not spook any of the butterflies. Cory turned away from me, and there it was on the back of his baseball cap: a teal-and-black butterfly.

My smile grew and grew until I could feel my cheeks encroaching on the bottoms of my eyes. I placed my right hand over my mouth as a laugh burst out, and Cory turned around. He began to laugh with me and asked, "What?"

I told him the butterfly was on his head, and we stood there, smiling and laughing gently so we wouldn't spook the butterfly. It rested on Cory for what seemed like eternity, a very long time for a butterfly to rest where it had no nectar to eat from the flowers.

I asked Cory if I'd ever told him about a teal-and-black butterfly and my Mustang and my brother. It turned out I hadn't, so I told him right then and there, in the meadow surrounded by butterflies, while the butterfly rested on his baseball cap.

When I finished, Cory smiled and said nonchalantly, "That's really cool." If only he could have known what I was thinking at that moment.

I knew that this was a nod from Richard that Cory was the one for me. That he approved of Cory, that he knew Cory was good for me. I was already in love with him, and it was a different love than I'd ever felt before. After the butterfly landed on his baseball cap, there was no way I was ever going to let that love go.

My thoughts are blessed with birds and butterflies by day.

—excerpt from Richard's journal

CHAPTER 13

Sharp Top Mountain

Like Big Sky, I had been to Sharp Top Mountain's peak more than once. After our butterfly field hike, Cory and I began the new trail at the foot of Sharp Top Mountain. We wasted no time getting started, because it was a much tougher incline than the meadow hike, and our goal was to get to the summit and back before sunset so we'd have time to set up our campsite.

The day was hot and humid; the sun shone through the leaves of the trees, taunting us in what should have been our shady refuge. We were dripping in sweat. Halfway up the trail, I silently wondered how the heck I was going to sleep in a thick sleeping bag that night. How was I going to clean the sweat off? If it was going to be just as hot that night, there was no way I would get any sleep. Between the heat and the stench, our tent was going to be downright unbearable. I started contemplating all of this when the sky began to darken and raindrops started to bead onto the rim of my hat.

We both let out soft sighs and admitted that we were thankful for the little bit of rain, rinsing the sweat off of our skin and cooling us off. Thunder erupted, the sudden noise ringing in our ears, and a downpour came in sheets of rain that opened the sky entirely. We ducked under a large rock and sat there for a while, unable to pass the time chatting because the rain rushing off the overhang of the rock was so forceful that the noise was deafening. Eventually, once the rain eased up a little, we decided to continue our hike to the summit.

Everyone else must have checked the radar on their phones or chatted with the park rangers at the station below, because when we reached the summit, the downpour now a light sprinkle, the usually packed summit was barren. We walked around the top of the mountain, climbing the rocks and hopping over puddles. We saw the rainstorm that had drenched us only a half hour before in the distance.

Cory effortlessly leapt up onto the largest rock on the summit, and then I followed, crawling as he reached his hand out to pull me the rest of the way up. We watched the rainstorm travel farther and farther away from us. A rainbow appeared, trailing behind the edge of the storm. I jumped off of the rock back onto the cement platform and grabbed my camera. I adjusted the settings on my camera and pressed the shutter button, freezing a moment of Cory sitting on the rock by himself, looking out over his shoulder toward the rainbow and storm clouds.

I set my camera down on a rock beside me, pressed the self-timer, and, in the ten seconds allotted to me, ran to leap up onto the rock with Cory. In midair, I willed myself not to go over the edge, believing that I could have that kind of leaping strength within me. In actuality, my leap was really Cory throwing his arm out to catch mine, and he pulled me the rest of the way, just like he had moments before. I fell into him, and our arms wrapped around each other's waists right as the shutter button opened and shut. We kept the camera propped up on the rock twenty feet away from us and continued to take in the scenery together, wrapped in each other's arms for a little while longer. We agreed that this summit felt special. Together there, it felt like it was ours.

Several years later, I found myself in the parking lot of the same trail with five other women, lacing up my boots and preparing to hike. Over the years, I'd learned firsthand what hiking mountains could do for one's soul. Richard had instilled this within me. I hiked because of him; I learned from him. And it brought me to this place in my life.

Unfortunately, I learned these things after he was gone. Although he is gone, his love for hiking and mountains has helped me see our world with a different set of eyes. And in this world, I have learned to cherish the ordinary, the small moments, and the smiles of others. I set out to bring others joy through hiking, and while I do, their joy naturally multiplies my own. I had planned this first hike on my brother's birthday.

This was the first mountain hike that brought my dream to fruition. For over a year, I'd wanted to build a community that uplifted each other, hiked together, and listened to one another. To laugh, to encourage, to empower; I wanted all of these things for the women who would come to hike alongside me.

The hiking community idea had been developing in my mind for over a year. But the journey to get there had evolved over the past seven years. In the end, my planning led me to this trail head on another anniversary of Richard's birthday, as I'd wanted to do something meaningful on his day. Something with purpose.

For some women, Sharp Top Mountain was the first mountain peak they would conquer. I had purposefully picked a hike with bathrooms, but since it was winter, I found them locked. After taking turns peeing behind a carefully selected rock—one we could confidently lean against while squatting, hidden just enough from the trail—we began our hike to the top of the mountain.

At the summit, we sat in a circle along the stone walls. Our 360-degree view of the rolling mountains and puffy white clouds couldn't have been blocked if we'd tried. As we pulled our lunches and waters out, Kristie shared her grapes with the group, while Holly thanked me for bringing us here today. I thanked her as well and shyly told them why I picked this date.

Erica, a woman who'd lost her mother to cancer a few months before the hike, said it best at the summit: "We all have different reasons for being here, to be hiking with one another, but it is great we have all come together for these different reasons." I'd known Erica since we joined the same sorority in college. Although our paths had taken us different places, we'd reconnected when she saw me share an open invitation to go on a hike. I was intrigued by this, knowing that she may be the first key to my idea of bringing something substantial to another's life. I could relate to her in the sense that we'd both lost someone we loved and were looking for a healthy outlet to grieve and ultimately heal. It felt like it was no coincidence that I'd created this group a few months after her mom had passed, when she began to search for somewhere for her energy to go.

The energy that comes from grief needs to be put somewhere, applied toward something. It needs to be released. Erica had long blonde hair, not yellow and not quite white, a perfect shade of gold. Since I'd known her, her hair had always touched her elbows. She was wearing her mother's hiking boots on that trip, and the instant she told me that, I wanted to photograph them. Normally known for being vociferous, Erica became quite soft in nature for a little while on the summit after I told her it was my brother's birthday. I imagined she was picturing her mom, with the same golden blonde hair but much shorter than her own, smiling and prancing around the summit.

Holly was a friend whom I'd met in the wedding industry, she a wedding planner and myself a wedding photographer. She was kind and joyful, and later on became known in our group for exclaiming, "This is the best day ever!" repeatedly while out hiking with us. On Sharp Top Mountain, Holly said to me, "Thank you for sharing his birthday with us." Then she tilted her chin up toward the sky and said, "Happy birthday, Richard."

I began to reflect on this moment even though I was still living it. Although the moment was still unfolding, I already knew that it mattered. We all sat in our circle, legs crossed and our knees touching. These women, who were strangers to my brother, were at the top of this mountain with me, taking a moment to say happy birthday to him in their own way. The other three women nodded toward the sky and raised their water bottles as a toast to Richard. All of us understood, whether we'd spoken up or kept to ourselves to ponder and reflect, that we were all on top of this mountain—at this summit—for a reason.

I hoped from the very beginning that hiking would mean a lot to other women. My hope and need for hiking to mean something substantial to others was both my foot confidently pressing down the gas pedal in creating this community and my foot switching to the brake pedal in a panic. I knew that this could really matter, and that was also what scared me about opening up.

Needless to say, when they all shared their reasons for hiking at the top of the mountain that day, the gravity of the moment overwhelmed me. I realized that my life was exactly where it was supposed to be. I was meant to press this gas pedal down to the floor. I was destined to give the love of hiking and adventure to others by inviting them to witness a mountain's power to heal and empower them. Richard would have been proud to spend his birthday the way we did today.

After these moments of Richard's birthday at the summit, we began to hike down. During the ease of hiking down the mountain, my mind was able to venture into thinking more about this community I had created and why. The infinite thoughts flooded my mind, like a random summer storm causing a flash flood that poured in seemingly unannounced, creating a rushing river in the middle of a trail. Like this newly formed and powerful river, my thoughts demanded my attention.

We all had our own reasons for lacing up our boots and setting out to accomplish something, and that's what made that day so extraordinarily beautiful. Everyone's individual reasons for coming on the hike had brought us together, whether it was a decision to spend more time outside or a promise to themselves to be more active.

If you want to get yourself out of your comfort zone but don't want to venture into the woods alone, if you've lost someone dear to you and are trying to figure out what your life will look like now, or if being out in nature with no cell phone service or WiFi just feels good, then hiking is for you. A person's reasons for hiking are personal, and no matter how big or small those reasons may seem to anyone else, hiking was for those women who hiked Sharp Top Mountain with me that day. Hiking is for you too.

When I find myself at the summit, my demeanor softens. My shoulders relax, and I marvel in the 360-degree view as the wind swirls all around me. I know that I am here to hike for a significant reason.

On top of the mountain with those women, a motto was born for all of us. To the women I have already met and all the ones that I will meet in the future, it goes a little—okay, a lot—like this:

Hike for her. She who believes that she can do anything, be anything; that's who you hike for. We all have our personal reasons for lacing up our boots and setting out to hike. Just like life, it's not an easy walk in the park, but also like life, do we really want it to be?

When you hike for her, you are searching for more than a walk in the park. You are ready to give her more, you're ready to shake her and wake her up. If you have not realized this yet, the her I am describing is YOU!

The best part in the unfamiliarity of the waking, shaking, and more is that you are not alone. You have others who made the decision to hike alongside you. As we dedicate ourselves to creating more for her, we use our hikes to build strength, determination, and friendships. We wake ourselves up to see new horizons, often before the sun rises. Hike for her, and I promise your life won't be a walk in the park, but a hike to heights you have yet to imagine. Be her, wildly.

CHAPTER 14

He Misses the Smell of Grass

There are countless scents and types of grass, and it's no wonder that I was once told that Richard now misses the smell of grass. Granted, a medium told me this. People can say what they want about their belief or lack thereof in mediums, but that statement made perfect sense to me. Wouldn't you miss the smell of grass? Something we take for granted every day, something that is always guaranteed to be there, surrounding us. We almost never go a day without coming across some grass. Something we overlook constantly, he misses most.

I found myself thinking, *I would miss the smell of grass too, Richard.*

I would miss the musty smell of wet grass after rain. The dusty scent of baseball dirt and grass being kicked up into the air. The crisp scent of a freshly cut lawn. The wild scent of overgrown grass in a field with weeds and wildflowers. The sweaty scent of the stains our mom had to scrub out of the knees and elbows of our clothes after we had rolled down the grassy hills of Mount Trashmore. The salty scent of a grassy patch that sprouted in the valley of a sand dune on Jockey's Ridge. The airy scent of grass that grows perfectly on the bald of a mountain, maintained by nature's elements and not by man.

I love finding blades of grass growing between boulders and in crevices; places we would not expect grass to grow, found where we would understand if it never flourished there at all.

I thought of this again as we approached the trimmed grass of Richard's childhood baseball fields. The grass curved effortlessly and perfectly around the dirt of the baseball field diamond. It was a cold winter day, the bitter weather perfect to give us privacy while we spread Richard's ashes. Dad started scattering them into the breeze. Dad stood at the edge of the field, and we watched him toss more of Richard's ashes into the air. The sunlight caught the ashes, making some of the speckles glisten and twinkle as they effortlessly floated down to the ground and settled across the orange dirt. Dad looked down at the ashes, and as we watched from afar, his eyes linked onto something in the dirt below him. It pulled him in like an anchor hitting the ocean floor, and as he bent down to pick it up, I wondered what he'd discovered.

Mom and I inched closer to Dad and glanced over his shoulder. A simple metal ring rested in his palm, and he traced circles around it with his pointer finger. Feeling us there hovering behind him, he said, "They told me the metal rings in his baseball cap may not melt, but I put one of his in with him anyway." I realized I was looking at one of the rings that borders the four air holes of every baseball cap I'd ever seen. But it wasn't just any metal ring, and it was not from every baseball cap we've seen before—it was from Richard's.

We had picked several places to spread Richard's ashes: Yellowstone, Big Sky, and multiple baseball fields where Richard had played throughout his life. Grass interlocks my childhood memories together like a familiar friend who's been welcomed into our family.

On this particular day, we were at the Great Neck Baseball Field Park, one that held so many family memories. To my left, I could see the hill behind the field, and I fondly remembered our picnics between double headers.

Standing there, I realized that I want to challenge us all to cheer for the blades of grass that we come across in our lives like we would cheer for someone hitting a home run in a large stadium. They are resilient and have survival instincts to flourish in areas you wouldn't expect. That kind of perseverance deserves a stadium cheering for it. I remember cheering like this for Richard when he'd smash his bat into the ball and the baseball would ricochet off and soar up into the sky and over the fence.

While we stood at the edge of the field, I pictured a ball flying into the air and everyone watching with anticipation to see if it would reach far enough. I remembered the hush that would come over the stadium as we'd wait, almost breathless. Then we'd all realize that the hit had gone far enough, that it was a home run, and for a moment, the world around us would explode in an eruption of celebration. He would run enthusiastically, rounding each base, proudly planting a dirty footprint on each. I could picture it all: the orange dirt still damp from rain the night before. The crowd's cheering, the sun shining down onto the field. I remembered seeing his number thirteen jersey dance across the entire field as he rounded third base and headed straight for home. Dad would proudly excuse himself from the stadium to search for the baseball that he wanted his son to always have. A memento of euphoria.

Our lives aren't full of home runs, but that makes those moments sweeter, more significant. Weddings are like that too.

When I started planning my wedding five years later, I wanted Richard to be with us in spirit on our wedding day. I picked out one of his home run baseballs from the bucket where my dad kept them and took it to a jeweler. They made the red baseball stitches and white leather into a bracelet for me to wear for my wedding. It was wrapped around my wrist all day, a whole city away from that Great Neck baseball field. I wanted Richard there in the gardens and fields of grass at our venue by the river.

I could feel him as the clouds dissipated, opening the remnants of the Nor'easter storm from the day before, and the sun came shining through just in time for our ceremony. The world seemed to stop with anticipation as I rounded the corner of the garden entrance with Dad, Vitamin String Quartet playing one of Sigur Ros's songs through the speakers. The train of my wedding dress brushed over the damp grass, my fingers intertwining with my dad's. At the last second, we had decided to hold hands across the lawn instead of interlocking arms. Holding hands felt right.

The tiniest line of mud rimmed the bottom of my dress when we reached Cory at the altar. On that day, the world stopped for us.

In an accumulation of years of healing and discovering myself after my brother was gone, his mark on my life became even more clear to me. As I reached out for Cory's hand, Dad shook his other hand and pulled him in for a hug.

Cory and I took out our matching notebooks and read our personal vows to one another. We marveled in the moment, taking our time reciting the words we had mulled over in our minds for weeks, the most perfect words we could come up with to promise to each other on our wedding day.

Our pastor told us that we could kiss and announced us as husband and wife. Our family and friends waited at the edge of their seats, and then, in our own moment of euphoria, they rose and gasped as we intertwined, then erupted in front of us. The pastor made a joke about getting us a room, and we laughed and turned to walk down the damp aisle of grass. The blades swayed under my dress, and Cory's feet proudly squished the grass into the mud, leaving his footprint—his mark—on our first married path together.

I have never hit a home run, but that day felt like a home run to me. I was home, and I understood Richard a little more because of it. I knew he had helped get me there.

CHAPTER 15

Park Ranger

I couldn't help but think, *If Richard had moved here, then maybe he would have been okay.* I thought this privately as I drove another car full of women into the mountains. That idea was sown into every stitch of my day, from the rolling hills to the small cabins peeking through the pines, the crisp air, and the open blue sky.

I saw Richard in everything. When I came across a park ranger—any masculine park ranger—with his back turned, my stomach would knot and a lump would form in my throat. This feeling never failed to rattle me. For a moment, I always thought the ranger was my brother, and I'd daydream that when he turned around, it would be Richard's eyes looking back at me, even though I knew that wasn't a possibility anymore.

On that day, as we pulled into the parking lot of White Oak Canyon, a ranger directed us to park. He looked happy, his laugh lines framing his smile and his wavy, gray-peppered hair curling out from under his cap. I nodded at him through my window and pulled into the gravel parking spot. The other women and I doused ourselves in bug spray and leaned against the trunk of my Jeep, lacing up our hiking boots.

The park ranger came over and talked to us, informing us that we would definitely need the bug spray, and warning us that storms were expected later. He asked us if we had hiked here before. When we said no, he lit up.

"Oh, well, you are in for a treat today! The water is still too chilly to swim under the waterfalls, but they are beautiful. Check in with the other park ranger right before the trail head, and have fun, ladies!"

I thanked him, and we set off hiking. Throughout the trail and over the creeks, I thought, *Richard could have done this and been happy*. Maybe in the balance of nature, solitude, and only a few people, his need for prescription drugs would have subsided. Maybe nature would have saved him. I wondered if one, just one, aspect had changed for him, and he'd stayed out there in the mountains, would he still be alive? Would he have found happiness?

I will wonder this for my entire life. The pit of my stomach will stay empty, and the wish that Richard had become a park ranger will fester.

It's not a far stretch to imagine this life for him, since years before, when Richard ran off and went to the mountains, something always happened that made him come back to us for a little while. I believed then that the mountains had saved him. In his absence, I could picture that his ranger life might have been like something out of a painting.

A painting from Thomas Kinkade came to mind, one that Richard had hung in his bedroom: a snow-encased cabin with smoke bellowing out of the chimney. The cabin was secluded enough for privacy, but welcoming enough to know that the man who lived there was ... happy.

Letting the chatter of the hiking women fade into the background, I quickly became lost in my own imagination. Pawprints in the snow led me up to the cabin's front door, and I figured there were at least two dogs here. The pawprints welcomed me enough that I felt confident knocking on the door, once and then twice. Before I could knock a third time, a man swung the door open and scooped me up, enclosing his arms around mine. Throwing my head back, I let out a laugh. I never wanted him to set me down.

Richard patted me on the back like I was his best pal, and his grin made my eyes water with joyous tears. He glanced at me with slight concern in his oak brown eyes, but quickly washed it away as two dogs came running toward us out of the woods.

Richard clapped repeatedly, almost cheering, as the two dogs swarmed around me, wagging their tails, whining with joy, and rubbing against my legs. I looked at Richard, wanting to remember his happiness, because although I could see every detail, I knew that this was a daydream. I recognized the dogs. Falling to my knees to receive the most anticipated slobbering kisses, I greeted our childhood dogs, Jordan and Windsor. They licked my face like I'd just come home after a long day. I remembered the days when they'd each passed away—Jordan when I was fourteen, and Windsor when I was twenty-seven—and I nuzzled into their necks. Windsor was a black-and-white springer setter, and Jordan was a mixture of colors, half Australian shepherd and half springer setter. They never knew each other, but in my daydream, they were the best of friends.

My eyes bounced back and forth from the dogs to Richard, who was holding his hands up to his mouth in a praying gesture and smiling through his palms. Finally, I nuzzled my face into the dogs' fur again and took turns smelling each of them. There was snow all around the cabin, but their fur kept me warm.

I longed to go inside and sit by the crackling fire with Richard. I could hear it inviting me from the porch. I wanted to stay for days, weeks, and maybe even months by the stone fireplace, wedged between logs holding up the cabin, having conversations with the man who could not stop smiling. I wanted to hear about his life and listen much more than I would speak. I wanted to stare at him and soak in the healthy glow of his skin even though it seemed to be the heart of winter. What park was he working at? What trails did he love most? Had he run into any bears like I had? What did he do? How was he feeling? When did his smile come back? How did he find Jordan and Windsor?

And finally, why couldn't it all be real?

Still entranced by my imagination, I subconsciously took off my boots and socks and dipped my feet into the water at the base of the rushing waterfall. The cold water sent a shiver up my legs and through my spine, bringing me out of my daydream and back to reality. I was at the base of the largest White Oak Canyon waterfall on the trail, and I was hiking with my group.

I knew that I'd been daydreaming. I knew that I'd had a real dream just like this daydream one night recently, but still, it was far easier to dream and believe than live with the reality, even if only for a little while. It was refreshing to put this fairytale in my heart for a few moments to suppress the dark reality. Because I knew in my heart of hearts that nature may have been able to save him.

As I balanced on a slippery rock, the water rushed over my feet, and I shivered unexpectedly. The air was warm, but the water was freezing. Every time I hiked, I tried to experience something new, using fresh eyes. I wanted to experience nature and life in its purest form, and that moment in the waterfall was all of that to me. That moment with the noise of the waterfall rushing down the face of the rock into the natural pool below it. Dipping my feet into the frigid water and feeling the rocks poke up and hit the bottom of my feet. The waterfall was magnificent.

Has Richard ever hiked here? Did he ever soak his feet in this water? Maybe his cabin could have been on the other side of this mountain. Looking down at the rock I was balancing on, I hoped that he'd stood on that same rock and stared in awe for a moment at the waterfall, because today, in that very moment, I got to do the same.

Oh, how I wished Richard would have become a park ranger.

Enduring love

—excerpt from Richard's journal

CHAPTER 16

White Oak Canyon

I turned into the familiar parking lot, which was marked by a Shenandoah National Park sign. Even on that hot and sticky July morning, the lot was filling up fast. Our group had chosen to hike the entire loop, all eight miles of it. I'd hiked White Oak before, but we'd only hiked four miles of the trail then.

Cory and I began the hike by meeting our friends, two other couples, in the parking lot. We doused ourselves in bug spray and strapped on our backpacks. It was an easy, flat trail with foot bridges over creeks through the woods for a mile until the first waterfall. We could hear the rushing water flowing down the rocks and crashing into the pool of water below before we ever saw it.

Once at the pool, I dipped my feet in, shivers creeping up from my toes to the base of my neck. The mist seemed to float in the air from the fifty-foot waterfall, defying the rules of gravity. With my swimsuit on underneath, I slipped off my shirt, shorts, and hiking boots and put them in a pile on a dry rock. Glad to be jumping into the cool, fresh water, I took the plunge. Trying to beat the heat, everyone else jumped in after me. We swam up to the rushing water falling down the slick rock face, and unlike some other waterfalls, there was no space between the water and the rock for us to swim under. The pressure driving the water into the pool created a strong current that prevented me from ever reaching the rock no matter how hard I doggy paddled.

Feeling much cooler, I put my clothes back over my suit, and we started the mile straight to the summit. Almost instantly, we were met with an intense incline we hadn't quite been expecting. Some of our friends wanted to turn around at the summit, hike down, and call it a day, but Cory and I convinced them to do the entire loop with us because we had two more swimming holes waiting for us on the other side, one with a natural slide. We assured them that first incline would be the toughest part, and I quietly cursed myself for wearing jean shorts, now all wet from my bathing suit. Soon I could no longer tell what clothing was wet from the waterfall and what was wet from my sweat. Jean shorts had been a horrible choice.

We reached the fire road, and our knowledge of all the fire roads we'd hiked on before had us convinced it would be an easy stretch to hike. A nice stroll was likely awaiting us until we would pick up the second half of the trail, completing the entire loop.

Our friends let us know just how wrong we were as we trekked through the rolling hills of the fire road. The little hills were deceivingly strenuous, and I was both shocked and amused at just how this wide, seemingly flat trail was conquering us. Our morale was withering, and each time we came to a turn, we told our friends it should not be too much longer, but every time, we were embarrassingly wrong. The length and progression of the incline tricked us over and over.

When our friends were almost at their wits' ends with us, they mimicked us, "It should just be a little farther," every time we saw a turn ahead on the trail. We finally came around the bend of what would hopefully be our last piece of the fire road. As Cory and I held our breath, careful not to utter our infamous words, we were surprised to see the trail begin to narrow. A new trail marker post extended a wonderful welcome to us. We reached the trail that would be our last stretch, and the post acted as a warm greeting to us as if giving us a wave. Pulling at my sleeve and then the waistband of my shorts, I noticed how uncomfortable I was. With all of the sweat dripping off of us (so much sweat!), I reminded everyone that we had at least one more swimming hole to find to cool off and wash the sweat off in.

The connecting trail immediately turned downhill, and we all took deep breaths in and exhaled sighs of relief for our legs. Hiking farther and farther down into the dense forest, we discovered the natural slide that I'd read about. Without hesitation, all of the guys ripped their shirts and shoes off and went directly for it. I watched them get on their hands and knees, asses in the air, and climb up the incline of the natural rock slide.

We watched each of them slide down and splash into the natural pool. I decided that I was going to slide down too.

But as I walked over, I got a better look at the slide, and it looked a lot longer and more treacherous than it had originally. I froze, feeling suddenly very self-conscious in my bathing suit. It felt like my feet were sinking into concrete, but when I looked down, I only saw my feet standing on the stone. I tried to talk myself into sliding down for almost ten minutes. I watched the guys slide down over and over again, getting their fill of the experience, and I saw my window of opportunity closing.

I finally convinced myself to slide down at least once for the experience, because my time in the mountains was about challenging myself and creating unique experiences. So, I climbed up the face of the rock in my one-piece bathing suit, wondering, *Oh God, who is disgusted right now at this view? I am never comfortable in just a bathing suit.*

I rolled my eyes and reprimanded myself, *Well, who the hell is, really?*

Step by step, sometimes placing my hands on the rock to balance, I crawled up the rock face and told myself, *Screw it! You are not going to miss out on real joy because you are worried about how you look!*

I finally reached the top of the rock and stayed low for balance. I sat down on the slippery rock face and pushed off before I had time to think any more.

As I slid down the rocks with my nose already plugged and my eyes closed, exhilaration ran through me! Sliding fast terrified me, but then I realized that with my eyes closed, I was not seeing any of it. I would only be doing this once, and that one time, I wanted to see. I opened my eyes, and just in time too, because I quickly shot off the sliding rock and splashed into the natural pool.

"I did it!" I exclaimed underwater, and bubbles rose from my mouth. I jolted my arm upward, willing it to find the surface of the water. Knowing where the surface was would have reassured me, because I had no idea how deep the natural pool was, and I wanted to come back up as quickly as possible. My hand finally broke out from the surface. My head followed, and then my mouth, which was ready to take a breath of fresh air. Once I took a few breaths, I blinked repeatedly and wondered for a moment if I'd lost a contact in one eye. But the truth was that at that moment, I didn't care if I had.

I looked back up at the rock I'd just slid down. I'd really done it, even after I'd debated in my head if I was worthy of the experience, the memory, because of how I looked in a bathing suit. How silly, right? What was important was that I finally came to my senses and realized if I didn't do it, I would have left the trail and regretted it the entire drive home.

These adventures are about me honoring my brother, and they are the complete opposite of regret. Without realizing that I was having an epiphany in the water, some children at the top of the rock were gesturing me to move along. I smiled because they were innocent and having fun without any insecurities or epiphanies. I turned and twisted my mouth into a knot, thinking, *Now, how to pull myself up and out of the pool on these slippery rocks?*

I ungracefully lunged myself onto the rock and scooted out of the way, imagining that I looked like a wet seal flailing its fins around just to get onto a rock along a jetty. I put my clothes back on over my drenched suit. With my soggy jean shorts scraping my thighs once again and my hair sticking to my neck, I hiked down the mountain without regrets—except for the jean shorts—but with a whole lot of memories. I noted to myself once again to never wear jean shorts while hiking. Seriously, what had I been thinking?

Near the end of our hike, the trail began to widen, just enough to walk side by side. Cory placed his hand in mine, and our fingers intertwined. He smiled and said, "I really needed this, this weekend." I nodded in agreement. I'd needed this too.

Bringing his hand to my lips, I smiled into his fingers, pressing down to give them a quick kiss. That loop had turned out to be one of the most strenuous hikes I'd done in a long time. Cooled off and relieved that the intensity of the hike was behind us, we began chatting again about things other than the hike. Our friends didn't seem to be holding any grudges. I joked with one of them about bears in the woods, saying I'd only have to be faster than the slowest person to get away. My friend didn't think my joke was too amusing, but I reassured him that I truly did know what to do—and more importantly what *not* to do—if we came across a bear.

Ten minutes later, on the last half-mile of our hike, as luck would have it, we came across a bear. We stopped stone-cold as we noticed the bear in the shrubbery off the trail about fifty feet ahead of us. My gut told me we would be okay if we just hiked closely together, making us look large, and made loud noises so we wouldn't startle the bear. The guys picked up rocks and rotted tree limbs, "just in case," as they told us girls. I rolled my eyes because we didn't need rocks and sticks, not only because we would not be fighting off the bear, but also because the rotted tree limb would crumble and do nothing but enrage the bear. I knew that black bears were the least aggressive, only charging when they felt threatened or if they had cubs with them.

The bear seemed to be alone, and sounds of thunder indicated that a summer storm had popped up and was quickly approaching our area. Our friends were not about to hike the nine miles back around, and I wasn't going to, either. There was nothing else to do but hike forward, past the bear.

The rocks did come in handy because we clapped them together and talked loudly. Everyone was tense, but I hung out toward the rear of our pack, watching the bear. I was sure everyone was doing the same, but their presence almost melted away from me. I didn't feel afraid as the bear lifted its head, saw us, and turned around. In an instant, it had run into the dense forest, away from us.

The size of its body bent all of the shrubbery in its wake. But with all of the dense vegetation in its path, the bear never broke the leaves off any of the shrubs. I never heard a twig snap under its paws. It reminded me of Richard bending the blades of grass as he ran his fingers through them in the ravine at Jockey's Ridge. The bear bent the plants but never broke them, and as it ran farther away from us, the plants began to sway back and forth. Eventually, we could no longer see the bear. The breeze it had created by running past slowed, and eventually the plants became still. They were stagnant in their original positions, leaving the forest with no evidence that the bear had ever been there. But I knew that it had.

CHAPTER 17

Humpback Rocks Hike

My cell phone alarm buzzed and chimed in the dark. The screen lit up my bedside corner, but otherwise my room was still dark enough that I could not have seen my hand out in front of me. I jolted awake, throwing my covers off of me and leaping out of bed to turn off the alarm. The only thing that could get me up and excited this early like a kid on Christmas morning was a hiking day. There was a chance of rain all day, but the group of women had chatted and decided that we still wanted to go on this adventure. In fact, I had planned another hike entirely, and I'd changed it at the last minute due to weather.

Forty-eight hours beforehand, I'd decided to change our plan because of the dropping temperatures and new flash flood warnings. No one would go swimming in the swimming holes on that particular hike, which was why I had chosen it, not to mention that a river and swimming holes made flash floods more likely. I often said "No rain checks" on rainy hiking days because I firmly believe in making the most out of the situation, but … flash floods … I'd go for the safer Plan B every time.

So instead, we traveled to Humpback Rocks, where we planned to hike 4.2 miles of the loop trail. We were immediately engulfed by the dense fog in the woods. The rain had stopped, but drops fell from the treetops when the wind lifted and swayed their branches.

I asked everyone what their favorite part of hiking with our group was. One woman said, "Getting out of my comfort zone." Many said things like the continuous laughter, making friends with complete strangers, and getting to know each other. A couple of women noted that they especially enjoyed when we reached the summit together and got to sit and enjoy the moment and talk more.

The list went on and on. Personally, my favorite part of these hikes is witnessing all of the different conversations, and how they come so naturally among these women who don't know each other very well. Each conversation almost always leads to lots of laughter, and everyone encourages each other throughout the hike.

I like to discover what everyone needs or wants to get out of each hike, and the answers are usually different every time. This group wanted fun, and they were adventurous! We pushed ourselves up the first mile of steep terrain. Reaching the summit, we climbed over rocks, each woman pushing herself a little out of her comfort zone in her own way. I watched each one of them laugh almost continuously while climbing around the mountain playground.

We had no view, but the fog made us feel like we were in the clouds. I suggested taking a photo of each woman on this one jagged rock that jutted out from the rest. They took turns inching out to the rock to sit, looking like they were floating in the fog that rolled in around them.

Each woman approached the rock differently to sit for a picture. A few chose to take one picture together, sitting down, maneuvering their thighs side by side, inching over to the edge of the rock. Another woman hugged the rock and threw her arms forward to pull the rest of her body along with her. Then she sat, hugging the rock to her right, the one that was closer to solid ground. I chose to walk out and then squat down, swinging my legs around to sit. I like to think I know when it's time to push myself a little more and when it's time to sit my ass down. This was one of those "sit your ass down" times.

Afterward, we looped around down the Appalachian Trail. My groups often hike in a single-file line or in pairs due to the width of most trails. On that day, I was not quite sure if it was the stillness of the fog and the cooler weather, but something inside me just wanted to observe my surroundings and the activity around me.

Stopping to take photographs of yellow and purple flowers blooming in patches along the trail where the sunlight shines through the trees, I naturally fell to the back of our group. This would have made me anxious a few years before. For a long while after Richard passed, I had a lot of fears about being "too sad" for my college friends. I was afraid they would leave me behind. Hiking in the back of the group today, I was confident that these women wanted to hike with me. None of that would have been possible without therapy.

Before Richard passed away, I'd begged my parents to go to a family therapist with him. My persistence got them there, although they needed little convincing. Their relationship was deteriorating with their son, and they wanted to do anything to repair it. They went with Richard a few times, but then he refused to go back.

My parents continued to go to therapy without Richard. They wanted to learn what they could and could not do to help my brother. They were also trying to cope even when he was still alive.

Little did I know that when I pestered them to find a therapist, I was also setting in place one for me over the course of the next five years. A few days after Richard passed, I went with my parents to see Dr. Siegel. Having never met him before, I asked them if I could go in for five minutes by myself. I walked in and sat on the right corner of the linen couch. I picked up the small, square pillow with its design that matched the couch and placed it in my lap, my right hand tracing the seam of the pillow as I began to open up. I remember telling Dr. Siegel that I did not know how to begin, but what I did know was that I did not want this traumatic event to ruin our family, our lives.

Soon after that, I began going to see Dr. Siegel alone. Twice a month over the course of five years, I would sit in the corner of the same couch in his office with the matching pillow in my lap. Fiddling my fingers over the seams of the pillow, I would slowly open up and learn, heal, and fight my way through the grief.

For one of my sessions with Dr. Siegel, I did not go to alone. A few months after I began going, my best friend, Nicole, asked to go with me. I was surprised, but a sense of comfort and relief washed over me because she was initiating this on her own.

What kind of friend asks you to go out to lunch and then a therapy session together? A best friend, a sister, one who does not leave, one I did not have to fear leaving. Naturally we had a fun lunch together, grabbed some coffee to go, and got to the parking lot early for our session. As we were laughing and chatting about how the appointment might be awkward and strange, I spilled my coffee along the length of my console. Upon searching the glove compartment and our purses, we realized that the closest thing to cleaning products we had were tampons. We stripped the plastic wrapping off and, one by one, we popped out the cotton tampons. I used all the tampons we had between the two of us to wipe up the spilled coffee. I cupped the coffee-soaked tampons in the palms of my hands, and then we jumped out of the car to throw them away and enter the building for therapy.

I sat down in my usual spot, pillow in my lap, and Nicole sat on the other side of the couch. Dr. Siegel had me chat a lot and then asked Nicole what she wanted to know.

Nicole asked him, "How can I best support her during all of this?"

This question enabled me to voice all of my fears about being sad and down for too long. How I feared that my friends would tire of me and leave me behind. Fear was loud for me for a while. I sat there in that corner of the couch for years, battling my fears. All kinds of different fears, old fears that would resurface and entirely new fears to conquer.

Yes, fear was loud for me for a long time, but it was only permitted to be loud because I had not yet learned that it was wrong. Our lunch, coffee-soaked-tampons clean-up crew, and therapy session date was one of the first pieces to learning that my fears would not win. That my fears were wrong.

Becoming present once again in my hike, I bent down and paused to take another photograph of a batch of wildflowers. It was the beginning of spring, and the flowers were beginning to bloom in small clusters. It was a little early in the season for wildflowers to be blooming, so I concluded that these must have been reaching for the sunlight just a little more than the rest. The rest of the plants were patiently waiting to burst into bright purples and yellows, but these first buds were eager.

Lush green fern leaves blanketed the forest floor. Their tips grazed the dirt, weighed down by the raindrops dripping off the trees above in the wind. I had never seen such a vast space covered by only one type of plant. The weight of the raindrops transformed them into one entity, pressing their leaves into one another to form a unified group.

A few times, I looked up from my view of these flowers and ferns through my camera lens and noticed the group was not in my sight on the trail again. I was confident that I would find my way back to the group because I always caught up to the group when I fell behind.

I'd gotten used to falling behind, expecting to always see the stripe of neon on the last woman's backpack through the brush and fog. But around the third time I watched that backpack disappear, without warning, my body jetted out from under me. I slipped on a rock.

In the air, my left leg turned downhill and took the rest of me with it. While I was airborne, I imagined the group finding me in a fetal position on their next switchback. My right leg swung around, following the momentum of the rest of my body, and my knee crashed into a boulder. The rest of my body flattened and hugged the ground below.

In my confusion, I deliriously thought about how paper covers rock in Rock, Paper, Scissors. I was the paper, and the mountain was the rock. Like a pancake, I slid helplessly down the side of the mountain, the mud seeping into my clothes. The mud first cooled my knees and then my ankles, pouring into the edges of my leggings and my socks. Instinctively, I dug my fingers into anything I could reach. I was truly morphing into the paper that covers the rock, only now I was a soggy, wet piece of papier-mâché, flimsy and delicate, clinging to the elements around me for stability.

Finally, my fingers grabbed hold in the mud, and I stopped sliding.

I called out, "Man down, man down." Of course, no one heard me. I knew what I needed to do next, and it made me cringe. On a previous hike, Erica had randomly bellowed out a certain noise to be funny, and the damn noise had stuck with everyone. She repeated it often, and the other women always followed suit, cackling over this noise. We all knew how ridiculous it sounded, but once that kind of ridiculousness was created, nothing could ever top it. We all knew to call out this noise if we wanted to rest or if something had happened and everyone needed to stop.

I sighed heavily and prepared to bellow out this loud noise from the pit of my stomach. Even in my time of need, I rolled my eyes. I'd have to be loud enough because I could not fathom having to do this more than once.

I reluctantly yelled out, "Caw, cawww!" like a crow. It sounded as obnoxious as I'd imagined it would. Instantly, I heard the chatter of the other women. I could not believe the call worked. However, they sounded far off in the distance, and I realized that, because of the distance between us, I would have to start to get myself out of this.

I dug deeper into the mud and proceeded to lift my right leg. A jarring pain jolted through my knee, reminding me that it had crashed into a boulder moments prior. I stretched my leg and planted my foot near my head, then repeated on the other side, crawling out of the muddy mountainside step by step. As I slowly got out of the mud and brush, I remembered an article I'd once read and sent to Nicole.

The article talked about how the dirt you get under your fingernails is significant. Looking down at my hands, the palm lines stained with mud and caked under my fingernails, I reflected on the meaning of the article. I swiped my left thumb through the thick mud on my right-hand palm, then inspected my fingers to get a detailed look at my nails. The mud, the dirt meant that I'd held on. It meant that I was there. The dirt was noteworthy. A reassurance that I'd survived. There was dirt under my fingernails, yes, but I was proud of the dirt because it meant that I'd held on.

As I stared into the dirt under the small white lines of my unevenly bitten nails, my mind drifted far past my minor fall down this mountain and back to all of my challenging experiences. I'd held on. We'd all held on in some way or another. That, my friends, is significant. Holding on—getting up—is always a conscious decision in life, and that is where the work truly begins for me.

Trying once again to clean the thick mud off my hands, then finally deciding the clean-up efforts were pointless, I shrugged, thinking, *Oh well*, and began my trek to catch up to my group. When I finally reached them, they all studied me, scanning me from the top of my head, slowly, almost sloth-like, down to my toes. I gave them time to take in my mud-stained knees and my drenched hiking boots.

They looked me over as I told them about my fall, and then we continued hiking as if nothing had happened. Just like that—like Nicole had done years before—they accepted me. They accepted that their organizer, their friend, had fallen. Once again diminishing my fears that often crept up about friendships, they all accepted that I was not the fastest hiker or the most outgoing of the bunch, that I was not perfect. Nicole had started showing me the proof that fear was wrong when I needed it most, and today my hiking group reminded me that fear was still wrong.

I carried on, chatting with all the different women in the group and rotating from the front to the middle to the back. There was no more mention of my fall, even though I was still embarrassed and continued to think about it for the rest of the hike. The pain in my knee every so often reminded me of my embarrassment. As we continued, we naturally fell in line with one another, interweaving our places on the path, hiking together. And although I was not perfect, they accepted me.

CHAPTER 18

We All Fall

There is going to come a time when you fall. We all fall. We know that we will get back up again. We know that we will be better because of it, stronger even. But still, you never mean to fall.

My story is all about falling. Falling and getting back up again. Bruises and scrapes decorating my arms and legs. The climb being stretched longer, further. You have read about a few of my falls.

Some falls can be funny. Some happen in slow motion. You may stumble, catch yourself, and think you have found your balance, and then you start stumbling again, belly laughing as your body hits the ground.

My dad and I shared a ski lift chair often while skiing at Big Sky. Getting onto the lift chair would stress me out on other ski trips as a child. I was always concerned about sliding backward into the people standing in line behind me. Or worse, pushing too close to the people in front of me and scratching their skis with my skis. Whenever I accidentally bumped skis with someone, they would shoot me looks that cut through me like the sharp edges of my skis.

If the line was moving fast, I would worry about keeping up, pushing my ski poles into the ground and pulling myself forward, dragging my legs behind me, hoping they'd trail along with my upper body quickly enough. The lift lines were always on flat spots, so I didn't have the incline of the mountains helping me.

After waiting in the lift line at Big Sky, eventually it would be my turn next. Standing shoulder to shoulder with Dad behind the thick red line, I'd prepare to start wiggling my way to the next red line to get my seat. Knees bent and ski poles tucked, I'd look like an

Olympian getting ready to start their race. Finally, the ski lift chair would swing around for the group in front of us, and we'd begin our wiggling hustle to the next red line as our ski lift chair whipped around the corner.

Don't fall, don't fall, don't fall, I always repeated in my mind as I got on and off the ski lift. As an adult, I gained a better grip on how to do this, but one day at Big Sky, the ski lift seemed to malfunction: as the chair whipped around, I looked over my shoulder, and it looked like the chair had whiplash, swinging side to side as it approached us. Dad unknowingly squatted to sit and ended up accidentally sitting in the middle. I faced forward again and tried to sit, but I landed on the handle of the chair.

Bouncing off the metal handle, I fell forward, and the chair smashed into the back of my helmet, pushing my face into the snowbank. Dad looked back, perplexed, as he rose higher and higher into the air, his chair still swinging back and forth. One of his ski boots popped out of its binding, and his ski plunged to the ground.

Still lying on my stomach, my skis spread out, wiping the snow from goggles, I watched Dad make a split-second decision. His body tucked and rolled to one side as he jumped off sideways from the ski lift chair into the pile of snow built up below him. As I laughed hideously and loudly, I imagined that the pile of snow he landed in had been built up right there for exactly this kind of thing. I was still laughing when he started laughing as well. We were both stuck on the ground, flailing around like fish out of water, unable to control our movements because our laughter made us completely lose control. My dad, a ski store owner, had intentionally fallen twenty feet off a ski lift chair. Luckily, we were at a lift to green trails, so the rest of our group never saw it.

A few years later, I was at Big Sky again. I skied down to a ski lift on the other side of the mountain with my husband, Cory. This was his third day ever clicking his boots into ski bindings and gliding down mountain trails, and he was doing a great job. He was practicing his turns and getting quite good at it. I loved the time I spent teaching my husband how to do something and having him rely on me to teach him.

We got down to the ski lift where there were more trails below and another ski lift off in the distance. This meant we had to turn to get into line, and we were up on a hill. This would have terrified me as a child. A thin orange fence trailed the edge of the hill, cautioning us not to ski off it. Cory and I turned into the line and stood there on our skis, plowing our poles into the snow to keep us in place as we looked up the mountain, watching for my mom and dad skiing down to meet us.

Out of the corner of my eye, I noticed my six-foot-three husband slowly get shorter and shorter. "Shit! Crap!" he exclaimed. As I turned to turn to look at him properly, he was gliding ever so slowly down the hill behind us, taking the orange fencing with him!

He finally came to a stop when most of his body had disappeared into the thick and soft snow. His poles sticking in the air, he began to laugh. I followed suit, unable to stop the tears running down my cheeks from the laughter. Shaking, I started to slide backward to the point where I almost joined him in the snowbank.

I caught myself before I met the same fate as Cory, and I enjoyed watching him try to pull himself out of the deep, soft snow, downhill, trying not to lose the skis he couldn't see but could feel attached to his feet.

We all fall. Sometimes the falls are hard, and sometimes they are lighthearted. Enjoy the lighthearted ones. Because when the hard falls come—and they will—the memories of those lighthearted falls will help you get back up. They will strengthen you to crawl out from where you have fallen.

CHAPTER 19

Yellow Jackets

Richard and I grew up on dirt. He found his love of dirt first, and I found mine second, with help from him. As we grew, our love for dirt grew with us, changing throughout time. Now I find myself loving places that involve dirt.

Crevices in the soles of my hiking boots contain a lot of dirt from different mountains, mud where I slid on a trail, pebbles that lodged into my boots. The dirt has crept up from beneath the soles to the toes of my boots. I laugh to myself whenever I think about this because I know that only happens when I slip or fall in the mud.

The hike at Nature's Cove was dry and sunny with lots of shade. We could feel the rays of sunlight through the trees creating warm patches on our skin. Summer was turning into fall, and the wild-flowers were still in bloom—but only in the patches of sunlight. I noted their perseverance against the cooling temperatures.

Our group was chilly in the shade and sweating in the sunlight. I am convinced that only the state of Virginia can pull off this kind of weather, and this is how it always feels hiking here at the cusp of fall.

Since I grew up on dirt, it never bothered me that dirt came with hiking. The baseball fields where Richard played had a lot of dirt. There was dirt on the field and dirt in the dugout, which led to dirt on the benches and the bleachers, where all of us would sit. We were so accustomed to the dirt being there that we never tried to wipe it off. The wind would kick up the dirt, or the kids would out of boredom when there were no base hits. I often dug into the dirt with the other players' siblings, probably inhaling dust whenever the wind kicked it up.

There was dirt in my girl cave, under the bleachers, where I often retreated with the baby dolls I insisted on bringing. I sat under the bleachers, where popping and crackling noises flooded my ears as people in the bleachers above ripped opened and tossed down peanut shells. I wanted to play with my baby dolls in the dirt, peacefully, and not watch *all* of the games! Even if I had to dodge all of the sunflower seeds and peanut shells bouncing off of my arms and legs, some catching in my hair. Nonetheless, I remember thinking I was so cool to be under the bleachers and not sitting on them with the adults.

Every day that we spent at the baseball fields, I quickly had dirt between all my fingers and toes. Baseball dirt is almost orange—especially in Virginia, where the dirt is pretty much just clay—and it stained my hands and feet like I had stolen my mother's sunless tanning lotion. It was in between my toes every day because I insisted on kicking off my shoes the second my mother turned her attention to the game.

I thought about the baseball dirt while hiking that day. I remembered once again how we'd spread Richard's ashes on one of the fields he'd played on as a child. How Dad threw the ashes in the air, how they glistened against the sun. One metal piece from Richard's hat had survived, lying in the orange dirt, telling Dad, "This one can stay with you."

On our hike, one woman pointed through the patches of sunlight in the trees to what looked like a bees' nest off the trail. We all nodded and agreed that it was interesting, and we were thankful it wasn't any closer to the trail. Our repetitive motions, one foot in front of the other on the inclined trail, made us all quieter because our bodies were working hard.

On group hikes, I often joke about the silence to the other women in between my gasps for air. Pausing between words, because I'm working pretty hard too, I say something like, "Woo! I love how we all become silent at this point! How's everyone feeling?"

They usually murmur back something funny. One time a woman told me flat out, "I hate you, Jessica," only to reach the summit later and say to me, "Okay, now this was worth it! I actually don't hate you."

I remember enjoying watching her take in the view from the summit. I'd known that she could do it, and she'd pushed herself to get there.

I got sidetracked and never made my usual joke on that day because I kicked what looked like a piece of the bees' nest that had broken off. Thinking little of it, my mind wandered back to the dirt of the baseball fields. I thought to myself, *Boy, do I remember the sting of a bumblebee!* Since I'd always kicked my shoes off at those games, I would run back and forth from under the bleachers, through the grass and down to the playground. Sometimes I would help Mom where she volunteered in the concession stand, swatting wasps off the candy and the counters that were sticky from the sugar of the sodas.

I cringed as I thought about the days when I had not been so lucky while running barefoot through the grass. More than once, I'd stepped too close to a bee and frightened it, so it had stung me. One time I stepped onto the pavement walkway next to the bleachers, and onto a squished bee that someone else had stepped on earlier that day. The stinger was somehow still pointing upright, and it went full-force into the bottom of my foot. Even in death, the bee still got its revenge on humanity.

People would bring me popsicles and bags of ice whenever I got stung, and somehow the popsicles made everything better.

It was mostly honeybees that stung me. I avoided the wasps and the yellow jackets. I'd always heard that those other kinds of bees could sting you more than once, though I always mourned a little for the honeybees that came in contact with me, stung me, and then died shortly after.

I chuckled to myself on the hike when I realized that I was genuinely mournful for the honeybees that had stung me as a child. All of a sudden, screams erupted from the two women in front of me. Instinctively, I ran, shouting, "Shit!!! What the Hell!!! Shit!!!"

The three of us broke off from the women behind us and ran. The woman behind me yelled, "GO! GO! GO!" Sharp pains peppered my legs and then my arms. Looking down, I noticed insects swarming all around me. One insect decided to fly toward my face, and I could see it line up with my left eye. It quickly flew too close to swat away, so I accidentally swatted it toward my face, causing it to sting me just under my eye instead of in it.

The other bees apparently liked this idea, and they collectively headed toward my face. I waved my arms all around with my eyes closed while running on the side of a mountain. I wouldn't say that is the safest way to run on a mountain trail, but I was desperate. Swatting the insects away, I hit the bill of my hat, and it fell to the ground. I thought about turning to retrieve it, but I settled with knowing that it was a goner and promising myself that I was not going to be a goner too.

We eventually stopped running and put our hands to our knees to catch our breath. Panting, I asked, "What the hell was that?"

Another woman replied, "Those were yellow jackets!"

My face began to ache, and one woman pointed at it and told me that it was starting to swell. Another pulled her pants down and inspected the welts that were forming all over her legs. We were a sight to see if anyone had come across us!

I pressed my hand against the welt under my eye. My eyelid was swelling, and I didn't know if I was allergic to yellow jackets. Bumblebees had never caused a reaction, so I figured I would probably be fine with yellow jackets, but I didn't know for sure.

Being unsure was enough for panic to set in. I realized that I had brought these women on this hike, none of us knew if we were allergic, and all of us had gotten stung. My face was swelling, and my heart was beginning to race. We were in the middle of the mountains, with about five more miles to go if we continued the hike. I remembered reading on the trail map that there was a smaller loop at a fork in the trail just a half mile ahead of us; if we took that path, it would be three miles back to the car instead of five. I apologized to everyone but told them we had to hike the shorter loop just in case any of us started to have worse allergic reactions.

I learned a lot about myself on this eventful hike. I learned that split-second decisions sometimes needed to be made, and I learned that I needed to be more prepared. I learned that although I had seen wildlife in the mountains, I was not prepared for yellow jackets. Yellow jackets, of all things!

I did not feel as mournful for those yellow jackets as I had for the bumblebees that stung me when I was a child, and maybe I should have. After all, they were just protecting their home, which we'd invaded. The stings were a significant and hurtful reminder that life was not always going to go according to my plan. Decisions would have to be made, and I might get hurt sometimes. I might fall ill. One woman did get sick, vomiting on the side of the trail about an hour after we got stung. Adventure may not always be a wonderful day without challenges. Adventure may sometimes be learning how I react in a crisis. Adventure may be the humbling reminder that this is the wilderness and we should respect it, because anything can happen.

When I was a child, I had the comfort of adults close by with popsicles in hand, ready to wish my tears away and bring a smile to my face. I also had the comfort of knowing that my pain was just a lousy bee sting. As an adult, I panicked, wondering if my throat was going to close up, because the worst sting I had was on my face, and it was swelling more by the minute.

I hiked in front of the group for a little bit, portraying the confident leader who would hike them out of this mess, and I began to talk to Richard in my head. He was the only thing that could calm me as I contemplated all of the scenarios that could happen, and I hoped that he could truly lead me. I hiked at a brisk pace, avoiding all of the sun patches that lit up the dirt trail because more yellow jackets gathered in the sunlight.

After some time passed and we were significantly closer to the car, I felt calmer. I was convinced that thinking of Richard and all we had been through in our lives, all of what I had overcome, had helped calm me down. I tried to make myself feel invincible even though I knew that none of us are, but in that moment, I needed to believe it.

Richard did not overcome addiction or depression, but I overcame being swallowed by his life and his death. I overcame heartache and mourning.

When we wanted to see change in the medical field, we were

advised that a lawsuit would get their attention more than anything else could. My parents and I decided to pursue this path, but it does not take away the things we have had to endure because of it.

With each step getting us closer to the end of the forest, the pain of the stings called on me to reflect on my involvement in the lawsuit. I remembered when I was summoned to come in for hours of questioning. My pain was great throughout my body while hiking, as well as in the conference room in front of all of the lawyers. They only suggested taking a break when my pain became apparent to them. Only after I began to cry. Hiking along this trail, I wondered if my tears had affected the lawyers. Maybe it had made me seem human to them. Maybe they'd realized that their job hurt people.

During a break in the proceedings that day, Mom and I were washing our hands in the bathroom. My sobs subsided as I ran my hands under the faucet. I stayed there, scrubbing with the soap that hardly made suds, and I lightly tapped the push-handle on the faucet to extend the water cycle. A woman with shoulder-length black hair approached my mom as she was drying off her hands and apologized to her, behind the door to the women's bathroom that hid us from the rest of the lawyers. She said that this was just her job.

We headed back to our seats, and I reclipped the microphone onto my shirt. The lawyers all began to dig in once again.

They asked me countless questions in the deposition and started calling Richard by the wrong name, so I stopped them. I was being recorded with a camera for the lawyers to review and prepare for trial. My new tattoo was itching my ribs, reminding me whenever I forgot that I had the strength of two people that day. I repeated the tattoo's quote in my mind: *Brothers and sisters know each other's hearts. We live outside the touch of time.* With my newfound strength, I stopped them and said, "My brother's name is Richard." I thought of saying so much more, but I held my tongue. When they continued to get it wrong, I repeated three more times, "Again, I can't answer that because you are getting his name wrong. My brother's name is Richard."

I overcame the lawyers criticizing me during my deposition. I overcame the anger I felt when they got a court order to read years of notes from my therapist. I overcame the vulnerability of knowing that they and their interns were spending hours reading these notes, highlighting what they thought could be used to attempt to ruin my family—or worse, ruin Richard's character. When they brought up the highlighted areas of these private therapy notes in my deposition, I overcame the disgust I felt at my privacy being stripped away from me.

On this nightmare hike, years after that deposition, I swatted yellow jackets away from me, and even though I was not always successful, I hit a few. That's all it took: swat a few, get through and out of the situation as quickly as you can. Some things in life you have to sit with to process and feel, but if you're in a hostile situation, get out as quickly as you can. I did get stung quite a bit, and it hurt. It ached. But I overcame.

Those lawyers hurt me, but I got to swat them—respectfully, of course. I was advised to be respectful and calm during the deposition. And though I never stood up from my chair, swinging my arms into the air like a giant flyswatter, I did swat them. I swatted them by looking them straight in the eyes, repeating my brother's name, and correcting them every time they got it wrong. Every time one of them dropped their pencil onto the table to try to distract me from the hush over the room, I never once lost my train of thought. I decided right then and there, looking into the eyes of the people who were getting paid to try to destroy us, that if I had anything to do with it, they would know who Richard was by the time I was done. They would get his name right.

I remembered overcoming all of this, and again, on the nightmare hike, I was reminded that I had the strength of two people. I was reminded of this combined strength on all of the days that I hiked, and especially the day when I was swarmed by yellow jackets. There may be patches of sunlight that are deceiving, unexpected areas where hostility lurks around the corner, like the patches of sunlight on that trail. When times get hard, I know I have the strength of two people, and I know I can overcome much. That strength reminds me that life has more beauty all around me and that it outnumbers those small patches.

We finally reached my Jeep where it was parked at the trailhead. It was in full sun, and more yellow jackets were resting on the tires, warming themselves. They didn't seem to be bothered by us. We jumped into the car, slamming the four doors shut simultaneously, just in case. We all shook out our heebie jeebies, and I threw my Jeep into drive. I smiled as my tires began to roll, thinking that some of the yellow jackets might still be on the tires when it rolled around to the ground. It was not my most mature moment, but considering my track record with yellow jackets, it was hard not to succumb to a little immaturity.

CHAPTER 20

Red Gatorade

Trigger warning! This chapter includes both graphic and abstract discourse on vomit.

I get carsick easily, which to me is kind of funny. I willingly drive on winding roads with hills that give me flutters in my stomach. When the front of my car tips downward, my stomach floats around in my torso. No matter how hard I try not to ride on my brakes going downhill or making a turn, inevitably I must brake, and my stomach lurches unpleasantly.

One evening, I met with a woman, Kristina, who was planning to book me as her wedding photographer. We had lived in the same neighborhood growing up. Her parents still lived there, and so did mine. Our childhood homes were on the opposite ends of the neighborhood. Hers was at the corner just before the lake and overpass of the main road outside our neighborhood. Mine was tucked into a cul-de-sac with a pool, where sometimes the crabs from the lake or the creek found their way into the shallow end. Maybe due to our age and our proximity in the neighborhood, we'd always known each other, but we had never spent much time together. Her brother, Anthony, had been friends with Richard. Maybe due in part to their older age, our parents had allowed them to wander a little farther than Kristina and I had been allowed.

Kristina spoke of her memories of Richard without ever mentioning his death. Maybe she was careful to avoid that subject because we were there to chat about her wedding day. I took a big gulp of my water to push down the lump forming in my throat as the thought crossed my mind: *Is it going to be brought up?* I was familiar with that particular anxiety, because when I would see someone from our past for the first time after Richard's death, the lump in my throat would always continue to grow until the subject eventually got brought up or the conversation ended.

While I was talking to Kristina, I brought up a memory about Snowshoe, West Virginia. Cory and I had been there earlier in the year, skiing and taking photographs of our friend's surprise proposal on the ski slope. I brought this up because I knew Kristina liked to snowboard. What I did not know was that for several years in a row, Richard had gone with her family to Snowshoe to snowboard. She laughed and told me about red Gatorade.

Kristina told me about the terrible winding roads along the long drive to Showshoe in the West Virginian mountains. Apparently, Richard had once puked up red Gatorade all over their car when the flutter in his stomach became too much.

I let out a laugh and said, "Gross! Of all things, why would Richard choose *red* Gatorade?" I was relieved that this had come up, because the lump in my throat vanished.

As simple as the red Gatorade story was, it was a memory of Richard that I hadn't known about. I'd never known that Richard went on those trips with them. I'd never known that he got carsick too. I'd never known that he threw up on people in a car in the mountains. And because of those things, I loved the disgusting short story she had told me. I love learning more about Richard, no matter how insignificant someone might think their memory of him is. I hold on tightly to each one I receive, trying to piece together his life even though I know, deep down, that it's impossible to do.

I'd assumed Richard had ridden along the roads to Snowshoe, but I'd never had a memory or story to place him there, and now I did. I cannot describe to you how that makes me feel, to be able to place Richard somewhere in the mountains where I had not been able to before, to know that he'd once occupied space there. It altered something in me, to be able to walk into a space that he'd once occupied and fill it. Like dropping a pin onto a map, I could mark this place along my journey. One day I will be able to tie a string to them, allowing all of the pins—the memories—to intertwine together.

Cory and I have a story all our own driving to Snowshoe. We were driving up together to ski with friends for the weekend. We crossed the West Virginia state line and started to sing the John Denver song: "*Country roads, take me home to the place I belong .... West Virginia, mountain mama ... take me home country roads.*"

Suddenly, the gas light lit up on the dashboard. There was no gas station anticipated for miles, but we finally came across a less-than-ideal spot about thirty minutes later. We pulled up to the vintage pumps that were decorated with rust. Hesitant, we observed our surroundings. Next to the building was a broken-down truck with several raggedy cats lying on the hood. They barely batted an eye as we got out of our car. The people inside the mart looked as worn as the cats, and I wondered if they were that way from decades of hard mountain labor. I speculated that the cats and the people might have lived just next door in the house with paint peeling off the sides. I wondered if the gas station was a family business.

I decided that the people were nice enough as I overheard their West Virginian accents in conversation. They barely noticed that I was there, giving me only the slightest nod as they carried on conversing. I even took the opportunity to use the bathroom, and I will leave that experience to your imagination. The door chimed as I opened it to step outside again, and I looked back at the cashiers and gave them a smile.

Cory was out front, finishing up with the gas. Once the numbers stopped dialing like a penny slot machine at a casino, he put the pump back in its place. We climbed into the Jeep and got on our merry way.

We quickly got turned around while trying to find our condo with no cell phone service and had to pull off on the side of the road. It just so happened we pulled off into an area that had one bar of service for my phone. Cory pulled forward slightly, and it became two bars—and then it quickly went back to zero, so I shouted at him excitedly to put the Jeep in reverse. We reversed slightly down the mountain to attempt to get the two bars again.

Eureka! We got the two bars, and I phoned the rental place. The chipper woman who answered quickly told me not to head down the mountain again, that we had been upgraded for free to the top of the mountain, and we would be getting a ski-in and ski-out condo. *Perfect!* We headed up the mountain, shut the Jeep off, checked in, and had almost cracked open two beers when we realized we needed to meet up with my dad's ski patrol friend to get our discounted lift tickets at his condo down the mountain.

Once we got back to the parking garage, I turned the key in my car's ignition—and nothing happened. I tried again to get the car started, and the engine made an angry noise, hissing and grunting at us. I switched off the heat and radio and tried again.

After a few more seconds of questionable noises, the engine roared on. I glanced at Cory and thought, *Oh crap!* We were not strangers to car trouble on mountains with no cell phone service. I inched my way down the mountain to this guy's condo, and we kept the Jeep running while we went inside to get the lift tickets.

Dad's friend chatted with us for about thirty minutes, and we never had the heart to tell him about our car trouble. After all, he was giving us a really good discount on the ski lift tickets. Finally, we walked back out to our humming engine, then crept back up the mountain road in the dark. I thought about that John Denver song again, and we jokingly sang to our Jeep in tune, "Get us home; you can do it!"

Turned out, the gas station with the raggedy cats and one gas pump had low-quality gas. It made me laugh; who would have thought? Clearly not me. As for the Jeep Richard rode in, I have always thought of puke as a domino effect. When we were children, Richard and I both puked on a deep-sea fishing trip with our babysitter. I still don't understand why she was thrilled about taking us on that trip. Who would take two elementary aged kids deep-sea fishing?

I've always thought that seeing someone barf is enough to make you vomit also. Richard's first puke—before I started—was the worst. And it is the sole reason why I believe in the domino effect. We were in a cafeteria-like area inside the boat. I remember a vending machine and tables and chairs that made me think of '90s fast food restaurants, the chairs scraping loudly against the linoleum floor.

Richard stood up to find his way to the bathroom, mentioning that he did not feel well. He stumbled with the rocking ship, swayed left then right, and without warning, hurled out vomit from the depths of his stomach. That was all it took to start a chain reaction in me. Richard swayed back and forth in the center of the cafeteria, instantly increasing my nausea.

On that fishing trip, Richard and I took turns lying on benches and waking from our attempts to sleep it off with lunges toward the sides of the boat to hurl our bodily fluids into the ocean. I remember throwing up on someone's fish as they were reeling it in.

Our poor babysitter. Kristina's poor family, who had to endure the puke-soaked seats stained in red and the smell on the long, winding road up to Snowshoe.

Kristina told me that once he was at Snowshoe, Richard had a wonderful time snowboarding with Anthony and his family. They quickly moved on from the uncomfortable. I am sure Richard felt terrible about what he'd done as his stomach settled, and knowing him, I can picture him cleaning their entire car once they arrived.

They all moved on from the red Gatorade. They overcame it, and from what Kristina told me, no one else got sick. In this case, there was not a domino effect, and this is what I want to remember.

Something unplanned happening that throws you off course does not mean that more bad things will happen. If one thing erupts in one seat, an adjacent corner, or another location, that does not mean that something in the next seat, corner, or location will erupt too. The situation does not have to explode. We have the option to resist the domino effect power when one bad thing happens. We have the option to try to overcome. If someone does something to wrong us, we have the choice to try forgiveness.

I won't deny that it will take work to clean off the vomit from our shirts or the car seats, dealing with the stains it leaves. But we do not have to hurl too. If the barf is on our seatbelt, it does not mean that our seatbelt will come unbuckled. We won't necessarily be flung around the car, bouncing off every area the puke is touching, getting covered in it or even injured. We can remain buckled and safe. We can still reach our destination and recover the rest of the day, weekend, week, year—our lives.

We have the opportunity to learn from the puke, no matter how unpredictable it is. We have the opportunity to forgive the person who got sick in the first place and sit with them while they try to feel better. If they do not get better, we know that it was not because, at first, we flinched at the act of puking.

Know that you—me—we all can get through whatever happens on our drive … on our journey in life. We can learn and become a better person so the next time someone throws up in our car, we can console them better. We will be able to understand just a little more, and maybe that is all they will need. A need to be understood. To be told that they will be okay. Ultimately, for someone to believe it for them.

Clearly, I am not talking about Richard throwing up red Gatorade anymore. I'm talking about life—his life—our lives. But please, please take these words of advice seriously, especially if you are going on a road trip with me: *For the love of God, drink the Frost Gatorade!*

CHAPTER 21

Abyss

The first time I saw an abyss—I mean *really* saw one—was at Big Sky. Every time I'd read or heard others talk about an abyss, it always had a negative connotation. People describe abysses as dark, bottomless pits of sorts. My experience is different.

Dad and I were riding up the creaking tram to the summit of Lone Peak. The face of the mountain taunted us, nearly grazing the tram as we got closer to it second by second. Everyone in the tram grew quiet. The only noise was the creaking plastic windows bending to the altitude change. I decided to turn around to another window to take my eyes off the face of the mountain.

That's when I saw right into the pure white clouds of my first abyss. I felt alive. I was in awe of the abyss, and anytime something stops me in my tracks with awe, I pay attention to it. Maybe that's because Richard described a waterfall to me one time, saying, "It stopped me in my tracks." He'd spoken of this waterfall as if he'd magically came across one placed there just for him.

Clouds covered the view of the mountain below. Everything underneath the clouds was blanketed by snow, blending into a dense, white landscape. The cable pulling the tram was the only thing noticeable amid the white, and eventually that faded into the abyss as well. The cloudy abyss was not bottomless, but what came over me was a swift, freeing sensation. My dad was terrified of heights, so he was uncomfortable. He refused to look as I gestured to my view, but I couldn't take my eyes off its beauty. I looked deep into the abyss, wondering if this was what Richard's entry to eternity would have been like. I daydreamed about how his eyes would open, and before they came into focus, he'd have been almost in a daze. Would his eternity have looked something like his favorite place in life at its highest elevation? I really hoped so.

We made our way off the tram and spilled out onto Lone Peak. Dad and I walked around together, not saying much to each other, but we'd both always had a mutual understanding. Dad could always tell what I was feeling but not saying, and I could do the same for him. We'd always understood each other. However, he made little comments like, "Don't go so far. Get away from the edge. Don't walk all the way out there." I laughed because he was at the summit of the biggest mountain either of us had ever been to, and he was afraid of heights.

While standing atop that summit, looking out over mountain ranges, seeing Yellowstone in the distance with my dad, I could never have imagined that we would one day return there again. Years later, we would stand there with my mom, who had overcome her fear of the trails that had stopped her from joining us the first time. She would be sixty pounds lighter, Dad would be more than one hundred pounds lighter, and I would look to my side and see my husband taking in the scenery with me.

In that moment on the summit, just me and my dad, I pondered the mountain ranges that lay ahead of me. I had no idea that over the next four years, healing, discovery, and purpose would all unfold.

The three of us had much to heal from, to learn from, and while I stood on that mountain peak, my heart was ripped open. Soon, it would start getting pieced back together, and the healing would begin. We were going through grief alone and yet together. Ahead of us, we had in store years of fighting for our lives and crying about our lives too. We would grieve and miss Richard. I would find solace in nature because, through everything Richard went through, his love for nature remained. When he lost everything else, he never lost his love for nature.

Closing my eyes, standing on Lone Peak for the first time, I thought about that fact: *Richard never lost his love for nature*. I felt the wind blow past me, tingling the skin on my nose and cheeks, turning them rosy and cold. The sensation of the wind sent endorphins through my body, and a smile appeared on my face. I vowed that day on Lone Peak to always love nature. I vowed to always actively pursue it as a part of my life.

Four years later, I was a newlywed, and Cory and I were on our first week-long vacation as a family with my parents. Bringing Cory to Big Sky was the closest I was ever going to get to introducing him to Richard. Cory got on his first pair of skis that week, which I described earlier. By the last day of our trip, we'd decided to ski into the bowl of Lone Peak, with its decorations of "Warning: Avalanche Zone" signs glaring at us as we passed them by. I felt like I was the only one whose stomach got lodged in my throat because of those signs!

Cory was ahead of me; John, the family friend who'd pointed out all of the bald eagles to me years prior, separated us. Dad was close behind me. I worried I would either pass out or throw up from worrying that I may get covered by an avalanche or one of us would get hurt some other way. It didn't take long for the fear of the unknown to begin to cloud my entire experience. We traversed in the ski tracks of previous daredevils that had come before us to where we wanted to drop into the bowl. As we moved, Cory disappeared and reappeared from my sight numerous times, following the daredevils' tracks up and down different snowbanks, tracks we couldn't quite make out until we were right on top of them. Everything was white.

In the sea of white, I decided my goggles were utterly useless. I peeled them off and put them on top of my helmet, and somehow the snow became even less dimensional than it had been. Trying not to panic, I quickly pulled the goggles back over my eyes. As my skis dipped down into a hill along the traverse, I worried that I would plow into a snowbank and become covered. When I was almost certain I was going to disappear, my skis took a turn toward the sky, and my body followed, reaching the top of the snowbank. Miraculously, my skis stayed on the daredevils' tracks. My stomach lifted like I was on a roller coaster, and for a moment, instead of knots and nausea clouding my experience, I felt exhilarated.

My eyes opened with the realization that the experience, knots and all, deserved to be felt to the fullest. Overwhelming emotion came to the brinks of my watering eyes as I looked around at Cory, John, and Dad. For the first time on that traverse, I truly saw it: another experience that I was gifted with. John ushered me to drop into the bowl, and I turned my skis down the mountain. Suddenly I was making turns and getting farther and farther away from a possible avalanche.

The fear was still in the back of my mind as I watched Cory ski just ahead of me. As I stopped to meet him halfway down the bowl of the mountain, he said, "I have nothing to look at to make my turns comfortably."

"I know, me too," I agreed. "Everything is white, but we just have to trust our skis. Do you want me to go ahead the rest of the way for you to follow?"

Cory nodded, and with a smile, I turned my skis once again down the mountain. I went slowly so Cory could easily follow, but also so I could remain in control of my skis. I realized that I had grown to be able to take the lead sometimes. I had fears—we all do—but I could also overcome them and help others as they needed. Cory always makes me feel safe, and I always have someone to help me through life. During that week of skiing, I was able to be that person for him.

At the bottom of the bowl, when we were well past the avalanche area and close to the ski lift, I motioned for Cory to pause. "Look, we did that!" I exclaimed. We spent a few minutes looking up at the bowl of Lone Peak in silence, smiling.

Later, we rode the same tram I had four years before with my dad, but this time we had Cory with us, and my mom met us there.

Once out on the peak, Cory and I decided to trek up to the tip of the summit together. We dug our heels into the snow and used our poles to pull us forward. This was where Dad had called me back years prior. Together, Cory and I reached the official summit, where the manifest of Lone Peak was kept.

People who reached the summit could write their names and a short message in the manifest—basically a giant notebook—to commemorate the experience. The manifest was kept in a metal box supported by two metal poles. At the foot of the poles, visitors could see a wrought-iron circle and triangle representing a mountain peak—Big Sky's logo.

We stuck our ski poles—which we'd been using as trekking poles—into the snowbank beside the box. I opened the lid and saw a notebook inside with pens and markers scattered around it. Others who had visited before us had written messages or drawn pictures. Some children had doodled abstract sketches, and some groups had come to Big Sky to ski together and signed it together. I knelt down, crunching the snow under my knees, and my ski boots slid out a little under my legs. Side note: Ski boots are hard to maneuver around in when they are not attached to skis.

I grabbed a pen and wrote: "Cory & Jessica Chenard in honor of Richard Fee 1/8/18."

I motioned to Cory so he could see it, and he smiled at me. We sat down on the snow near the manifest. Cory took my picture, and I took one of him. Finally, we just sat and looked out over the mountains and clouds. They seemed to go on forever.

Taking in the view, I noticed my dad about fifty feet below the hill we'd trekked up to the official summit. He was looking out over the mountains before us as well. His arms were spread out wide with a ski pole in each hand, undoubtedly pushed firmly into the ground because of his fear of heights. He was very easy to spot in his bright orange ski pants. Naturally for me, I took my phone out to photograph him with the mountains. A sun flare appeared a few feet away from him in the photograph, and I froze them together in time with the press of a button. I smiled and put my phone away, closing the pocket's zipper.

On our last day at Big Sky, we had a pizza party with Dad's ski shop group. I told him about the picture I'd taken of him. He told me he had been thinking of Richard during that moment alone on Lone Peak. This didn't surprise me; I'd known then, even fifty feet above him, that he was deep in thought, processing his own time on the peak of the mountain. I'd known that he was a father thinking about his son.

As I watched Dad mingle with the group, a piece of a wood log broke off from the heat of the fire in the stone fireplace. It sent red-hot embers soaring up the chute. Dad smiled across the room and glanced around at the group he'd brought there. They were all taking turns reminiscing about their individual weeks of skiing. I noticed something new in the way Dad was standing, in his demeanor, in the physical changes to his body. He was taller, lighter, and brighter—and no, he wasn't still wearing his bright orange ski pants. Now he was brighter on the inside, only his eyes telling the entire story of his journey, and only to the ones who were closest to him. He had come a long way since the last time we were first on that peak together. We all had.

Deep abyss—beyond abyss

—excerpt from Richard's journal

CHAPTER 22

Yellowstone

On another day on that trip, we took a break from skiing and traveled over to Yellowstone to snowmobile. The snowmobile tour guides handed us snowmobile suits, all black with neon stripes down the sleeves, down the legs, and across the chest. The neon green block across my chest read "Arctic Cat," and a large black belt fastened around my waist with a plastic buckle. A guide handed me chunky boots, thick gloves, and a skull cap. While I put each item on, I could feel the sweat building in the small of my back. I was momentarily transported back to the slow-motion movements Richard and I had made in our front yard as children because we were dressed from head to toe in layers for a mere three inches of snow. This confinement as an adult instantly made me feel like a child again, like the little boy from *A Christmas Story* who can't put his arms down. I laughed at the restriction of my limbs as I took crunchy step after step toward our snowmobile.

I went to swing my leg over the seat of the snowmobile, and it quickly fell back to the ground. It wasn't from lack of effort, but from the weight of the clothing and the boots. I bent the best I could at my waist and hooked my left leg with my arms, under my knee, tossing it over the side of the snowmobile. Finally, success! I was on the snowmobile and ready to go!

The rumble of the snowmobile engine was deafening until I got used to it. I'd have thought that the animals in Yellowstone would run far from the roads at the first sign of us approaching. But they didn't care; over a foot of snow had fallen in the park in the previous forty-eight hours, and they wanted to travel on the packed-down snow because it was easier on them. Our snowmobiles were only a nuisance, and they seemed to know we would not harm them.

We saw a few bison in the road here and there. I hoped to encounter a herd of them on the road so we could slowly make our way through. I was clutching Cory's back to stay safely on the snowmobile.

We sometimes stopped to walk the trails to see the thermal features and the clay pots bubbling up in their thick mud, and afterward, we'd get back on the road with our snowmobiles. Soon, our guide signaled for us to slow down and cut off our engines. I scanned the horizon line ahead to see why we'd stopped, and then I saw him: a bushy-tailed coyote. It paused, looking at the tree line, then at our mobiles, and back at the tree line. Then it started to walk down the road toward us.

I quickly pulled my cell phone out to take photographs. As I snapped a few, I looked over my phone and directly at the coyote. This was something I wanted to see fully, and not exclusively through my phone screen. After I got a few pics, I put my phone down.

We were all silent as we waited for the coyote to decide to disappear into the trees. It paused for a moment across from each snowmobile, then kept walking down the line, their paws pressing into the fresh snow with each step, all of us silent enough to hear the crunching. When it approached us, it raised their head slowly and carefully toward us, and I made eye contact with it. It paused again before picking up and putting down its right paw. The crackling snow gave way to make its print, and it repeated with its left paw, and then the hind legs. It looked back over its shoulder once more before it scampered off into the trees and out of view.

The coyote seemed like it wanted to linger there with us, watching us carefully, but knew that it eventually needed to move on. After years of my grieving Richard, this one coyote mirrored how Richard must have felt going into heaven. Maybe Richard lingered with us for a while, looking back, keeping a watchful eye to see where we were and what we were doing. Careful with each step, he left his mark on us. Then, when he felt it was time to fully cross over, he glanced back at us one last time, then walked off into the snow-blanketed land. He walked toward the horizon until we could no longer tell him apart from the snow he walked on.

Gripping Cory's shoulders, I looked around and talked to Richard in my mind, truly seeing how he was a part of everything there. I smiled, loving the idea that he had once snowmobiled out of Yellowstone like we were doing now, that he and I had both witnessed the same sun set behind the same mountain and its golden light reflecting off of the same river, and that reflection had shined up onto his face as it had done mine this evening.

We'd set Richard's soul free on those mountains. And I couldn't help but experience that freedom with him as the wind whipped past me and the snowflakes caught in my hair, as the coyote greeted us and spent time with us. As Old Faithful erupted, shooting steam and boiling water from the ground into the air. As bison lifted their heads from burrowing in the snow to reach the grass as we drove by, and as bald eagles soared above us. It was all Richard, and all of it was free.

As I've gotten older, I keep his memory alive by loving the things he loved. In doing that, I have come to realize something bittersweet. We would have been best friends by now, not just brother and sister. I will always look at Yellowstone and Big Sky and think of Richard. I will always look at an empty ski chair as it passes me by at Big Sky and wonder if he sat there, and I will always do things in honor of him. Because I love to. Because it comforts me. Because it sets my soul free when I come to visit his.

CHAPTER 22

Hawksbill Mountain

There are notable times in my life that led me here. All trails lead somewhere, and while I began on a very uncertain path, it continuously led me to new ones. Losing Richard led me to Big Sky. Big Sky led me to loving nature, which led me to exploring trails in Virginia and eventually to meeting Cory. This took me to new trails, where I created new dreams. One new trail encouraged me to create my hiking group, organizing hikes for myself and other women, inviting them to come hike alongside me—and then yet another trail helped me decide to write about it. All of it. All of the trails led here, and they are continuously leading somewhere new.

I prepared my peanut butter sandwich like I do the night before each hike. I got up the next morning at 5:30 a.m., half awake and fumbling for things in the dark while trying to not wake up Cory or our dogs. The less I have to do in the morning, the better.

I packed up my backpack with several waters, Clif Bars, and my peanut butter sandwich in one pocket. The back pocket held my camera, my camera lens, and an extra layer in case it got cold or rained. As I drove to meet the hiking group in Newport News for our carpool, I thought about how the hiking group had grown over the past year and a half. We had a few carpools coming from different cities: ours from Newport News and others from Fairfax, D.C., Richmond, and Gloucester. Seventeen of us were meeting that day to hike the Appalachian Trail to Hawksbill Mountain.

I needed that hike that day. I had needed this hike badly for about a month. My hope for every hike was that the women who came with me would get a lot out of being together, even if they didn't tell me all of their reasons for hiking. My reason for hiking on that day was that Cory and I had been trying for several months to start a family—unsuccessfully.

I hadn't seen this stage of my life coming. I hadn't thought I would be so impacted by not getting pregnant right away, but I still saw hope, and I could still picture myself summiting mountains with Cory, kids strapped to our backs. I could already picture looking back on that part of my life and thinking, *Good thing you didn't lose hope. If only you could have seen how close the next part of your life truly was. Only a couple of switchbacks, and it would be there. You could almost touch it; you just couldn't see it yet.*

It was raining and foggy during the entire hike. Luckily, the trees protected us from the heavier raindrops, and though everything was wet around us, we were able to stay dry for the most part. I hiked primarily with two pregnant women. I was naturally drawn to them, wanting comfort and hope from them. I wanted to hear their experiences. I wanted to know that I was not the only one to struggle. Through switchbacks, over wet rocks, and through the trees, we chatted about all of our excitement and fears about becoming mothers, and the new phase of life they were both in as they uncertainly awaited being a first-time mom. They grew my hope for the possibility of becoming pregnant because they related to my fears and excitement simultaneously.

I was not yet a mother, but I so wanted to be. I relished the possibility that everything might change but knew that my dreams would still be accomplished. For a long time, adventure to me meant trips and summits, but I now imagined that it could also mean motherhood someday. My personal definition of "adventure" is constantly changing, morphing as life moves forward. I am morphing, and I believe that is what we are all meant to do.

Adventure can be weeklong ski trips, hikes every month with other women, camping a couple times of year, and traveling to new places. It can also be the daily adventures of building a life, a home, and a passion. Adventure can be accomplishing something or simply practicing something, the way I make the conscious effort to keep writing.

Adventure is me writing this story because it pulled at my heart, begging to surface. Adventure is living day-to-day life with my loved ones, always building on love and happiness. I love mountains, but adventure isn't always about reaching the peaks.

Adventure can be the beginning, where I have to make the decision to simply start. It can be the valley, the hike along the way that is not quite picturesque. It can be the middle of my trek, when I do not know what is around the corner. If only I could peek around that corner first; how much easier it would all be then. But all I know is that no matter how hard I try, I cannot peek around the corner to see what the future holds. I can only put one foot in front of the other and be present in the adventure I am currently on.

Even if I think things are getting mundane or I'm not where I thought I would be at any given moment, every day is my adventure. It's my life! I don't want to worry about what's around the corner or the next summit or the summit after that, because I may forget that I am on this summit, in the valley, or maybe somewhere in the middle of my journey right now. Regardless of where I am, my adventure is now.

My everyday adventures are going to be what I remember most, and I want to bask in them. I do not want to take these days for granted. I will live in the moments along the trail with my friends and family, and I will continue to do the adventurous things that make me happy until my adventure changes to a different one. No matter what happens, I will never forget that I am always on an adventure.

If I could give any words of encouragement to the women who hike with me, I would tell them to try not to lose sight of the adventure they are currently on. The uncertainty is there, the future is unknown, but each step you take forward is a step in the right direction. Your path is your adventure; trust that you are on the right one.

There are so many corners we cannot see around, but our adventure is already here. It will have many corners, switchbacks, and countless trails to embark on. And as we walk along those trails, they shape and mold into moments we will cherish. It's all here; we are already here. Try to refrain from spending your entire life trying to grasp onto what you cannot see around the corner. Feel and view what is currently in front of you. Be it a valley or a summit, take in this moment. Welcome to your adventure!

CHAPTER 24

Skyline Drive

For a long time, I questioned what I truly needed in order to build a successful community for hiking and writing. I wondered if I was the kind of person other people might think would lead a hiking group—or write a book, for that matter. Would other people think I didn't fit the bill? I quickly learned that I was asking the wrong things. I realized that success is all about how you choose to define it. Your level of success depends on how you want to live your life; the bar of success is your own to raise. It took a while for me to fully grasp this.

I am not a body builder, a marathoner, or a size two. I face challenges on every hike, and I like to think they make me more approachable. I get out of breath, I sweat, and I take breaks. Sometimes I take a break for water, and sometimes I disguise my breaks as wanting to stop to photograph something.

I'd just finished hiking through the meadow across from the Big Meadows campground. I walked back to my Jeep and continued on with my plan to drive down Skyline Drive, stopping along the way where I wanted to. I took my time driving, thinking about all sorts of things. I thought about my writing and my dream of being a published author. I wanted to tell this story of how I climbed, clawed, and pulled myself up onto the top of the mountain. I realized that when it comes to my dreams, I'd been asking the wrong question: *Why me?* So instead, I asked myself a better one: *Why not me?*

My response to my own question went a little like this: *Exactly! No one decided it wouldn't be you except your own doubts. This is you, so embrace it!*

For a long time, I often downplayed writing, never telling most people how my heart ached when I had an idea for writing, how I would let the concept sit for a while. Eventually, the words would begin to stir until their force erupted, and I had to write. My feelings and words, my pain and hope all collided. I realized over and over again that my pipe dream was actually my *calling*. I was doing myself the greatest disservice by trying to label my calling in the first place. When my writing erupted, I knew that it wasn't actually supposed to be all about me.

I laughed to myself as I pulled over at an overlook and picked a rock to sit on, journal in hand. I began to journal more about my calling. I wrote that we can give the most encouraging words to others, but when it comes to ourselves, we are the first to critique everything.

I want to be a writer, so I am. I write, therefore I am a writer. I want to write this book. Therefore, I'm putting time and effort into it, because *why not me?* I want to help others feel their dreams awaken and their confidence build. I want to see their eyes fixate on a mountain. I want to witness them learning from hiking to conquer what is going on in their lives and not just the mountain itself. I want their energy, their strength, their perseverance to stand for something once they reach the summit. I want them to bottle up that feeling, that magic, and take it off the mountain with them and keep it always.

I have been anticipating that I would have a revelation of when I was done writing, or that there would be a clear end to this chapter of my life. I imagined I would someday be one hundred percent healed from losing Richard. I imagined I would someday be done writing our story.

But I have come to this realization: We are not out here to conquer a thing completely and be done with it. I should truly have this memorized by now. Whatever your thing is, why wouldn't we continue to grow and learn from it? Life would be boring otherwise.

That is why I am never going to be done learning and basking in all the ways that nature helps and fuels me. I am never going to be done wanting to help instill this in others. I am never going to be done living in a manner that embraces life because I know loss.

I will never be done honoring Richard in ways he helped to inspire and heal me. The thing is, I never want to be done. I will carry a part of him with me forever. And in turn, nature and mountains will be with me forever. But the best and most healing thing about the mountains is I can physically visit them anytime that I want. I can't carry them with me, but whenever I need to come back to them, they are there. I can touch the dirt; I can pick up a rock; I can see it. I can place myself at the foot of sites to marvel in.

Richard is different—I carry him with me. And I come back to the places where I am lucky enough to feel his presence again and again, attempting to find a sliver of that same magic. Most times there is still a sliver, but I know I need to package it up and carry each new magical moment on a different trail with me. The carrying has become part of the magic. That's how I continue to grow, learn, and heal.

Twirling my pen in my left hand, I realized that I was meant to write about the trail magic there that day. This was what I'd come for, so I closed my journal and placed my right hand gently onto my stomach. Looking down, I told the little one in my belly that their uncle had instilled this love for nature in my soul. I told them I would show them those mountains one day. I assured them that whoever they would become, I would love them fiercely. They would experience adventure and freedom the way that only nature can provide it for us. I reassured the little one, and myself, that this world is good, and we had so much beauty to see together.

Standing up, I took one last look across the valley below and the mountains all around me. They were turning their magnificent shade of blue (they're not called the Blue Ridge Mountains for nothing). Photographers call that time of day the blue hour, which happens right after the golden hour, the perfect hour of light to photograph in. But the blue hour is after the sun dips down, and it's the last sliver of light of the day. Because rain clouds were rolling in on this blue hour, I decided it was time to head home.

I headed back to my Jeep, got in, and turned the key. My radio came to life, but I rolled down the windows and then decided to shut off the radio. I put my car into drive, drove out of the pull-off, and merged back onto Skyline Drive.

Sticking my hand out the window, I let the wind whip past and fill the inside of the car. I loved being able to hear the wind and let my hair be taken by it. I thought, *I don't do this enough.* A herd of deer were crossing the road just ahead, so I slowed down. I watched quietly as they traveled across the paved road and disappeared into the woods on the other side.

Accelerating at a straight part of the mountain road, I looked up toward the treetops and saw a hawk flying, the brown and white patches on its wingspan spread wide. I glanced down to the road and back up to the hawk repeatedly, not wanting to lose sight of the hawk but also wanting to drive safely. Suddenly, as if it read my mind, the hawk slowed and dipped down just below the treetops, coming closer for me to see. It flew for a while above the front of my car before it soared higher again and changed direction, flying over the trees and swiftly out of sight.

Seeing the hawk made me realize that Richard was not finished showing me life. And I was not finished sharing his with the world either.

CHAPTER 25

His Books

I pulled over Richard's camping chair and pulled the string that hung in the center of the attic. The lightbulb flickered a few times before lighting properly, acting as a spotlight in the otherwise pitch-black attic. My mother motioned to the boxes to my right, handed me a small flashlight, and then left me by myself.

Kneeling down on the plywood, I exhaled to awake the dust, spilling it into the air, and brushing the rest off the lid as I lifted it from the box. Rows of baseballs, trophies, and gloves layered the first box. Next, I started pulling books out of the second box one by one, scanning the titles, sometimes looking up an author with my phone. I traced my finger over the words Richard had underlined. I flipped a page and saw the word "wow!" written on the side of a paragraph Richard seemed to have been captivated by. I placed some books to the side to take home, and then remembered that books were not why I was there.

I'd come to my parents' attic to find Richard's journals. I'd been feeling a pull to read them. I believed there was something in them for me to find that would either help me better understand him, hint toward his love for nature and camping, maybe list some outdoor locations he'd loved, or clarify something for me. I am not sure what clarity I was searching for, because although he hadn't left us a note, I'd never felt the need for one. But now I was searching for something.

Next, I unearthed all of Richard's medical study books for the MCAT test. It was nice to see his handwriting again, in all caps, answering questions I didn't understand. I thought about it later and realized I was meant to find these items of Richard's in this order:

baseball items, books, MCAT study guides, and then hopefully his own journals.

This timeline resembles the way his life happened. Lucid, he'd answered complicated equations in his study guides, ones I surely did not understand. Then his love for writing and reading evolved, and ultimately his journals turned into fragmented thoughts that he claimed didn't always make sense to him. Reading through the evidence of this process, uncovering his choice of books, and deconstructing through his sporadic thoughts that became questionable even to himself at times—it all revealed his unraveling. I gathered that if there had been dates on every page, we would have been able to pinpoint when his addiction truly started to take over.

Thumbing through the study guides, I thought back to the day when Richard told our mother that he did not want to become a doctor anymore. She certainly had not been expecting that. I imagined her puzzled expression as she listened to his words: "Mom, I am meant for something more. I am meant to help and reach more people than I would by becoming a doctor. I want to be a writer."

Had we known the weight of what that statement would become, we would have moved mountains to stop it. Because the alternative, the one I much prefer, is that Richard would be writing this story himself. He would be the one reaching and helping. But there I was, in an attic, unearthing equations for mathematical problems I couldn't begin to decipher, still wondering a decade later—how did this happen?

In his medical books, I stumbled upon a section about the human brain. An instruction read: "Define anxiety and how it affects an individual." Richard wrote, "Increased heart rate, especially if you are a smoker." I sighed and wished that Richard had visited these mental health pages longer. If he had learned what a prescription drug could do to a brain when abused, maybe he would have stopped before it gained its avalanche momentum. The thing about avalanches, though, is you can't stop them once they start.

Experts can now suppress avalanches from occurring in the first place. Big Sky set off their own controlled avalanches to break up the snow to prevent unplanned avalanches from happening before the skiers got on the slopes for the day. I could hear canons going off every morning while we were there. Maybe the doctors could have controlled Richard's avalanche, breaking it up in pieces, helping him to get through the danger and stand up once again, dusting the snow off his shoulders, battered but not defeated.

Once when I skied the bowl, anxiety had crept up on me, and I actually thought for a moment, *Did I just put myself directly in the line of unnecessary danger?* Lots of people have anxiety, whether chronically or occasionally, and it happens to me too from time to time.

For me, anxiety happens because I am all too familiar with Richard's avalanche. I know the momentum of something barreling down toward you and feeling unable to stop it. I know what it feels like to have no control. I know his unraveling, and I know losing him. Fears seeped into my heart and mind about losing other friends and family. It made me anxious, to say the least.

I slammed the last dusty medical book shut and put the rest of the books back into the box. I closed the lid, frustrated that I was nowhere closer to finding what I was searching for. However, I was done in the attic for now.

I asked Mom if she would let me into our storage unit, which was only a few minutes away. It was getting later in the evening, so I promised I would only look through the first two boxes she thought his journals might be in.

We got into the car, and Mom drove us out of the neighborhood and across the street to the storage unit. She unlocked the door, and together, we pulled it up over our heads.

Mom pointed to two boxes in the corner that she knew contained Richard's belongings. When we opened them, it turned out that she had chosen correctly. Although it was getting later than I wanted it to be, we began to skim through some of the pages. One cover was etched with Richard's handwriting spelling out, "ILOVEYOUSTOP" and another journal had only one page of writing, which read, "Jesus please help me." I shut that book forcefully and quickly gathered all of them in my bag. I didn't want Mom to see that page. My heart sank deeper and deeper into my chest with every passing second, and I wondered if I was doing the right thing. I turned to Mom with a knot in my throat and asked her about the first cover: "Do you think that means he doesn't want me to do this?"

I knew in my heart that I would not share all of the details of Richard's journals with everyone. I would only share the parts that would help others, but I would never share every page word for word. I desperately wanted a sign that this infringement on Richard's privacy was okay, that he understood the importance of it.

I wanted him to know that I was only trying to help him live on and help others. I wanted someone else's sister to know what to look for. I wanted them to see a page in the middle of the journal that read, "Jesus please help me," in time to help their brother. I wanted them to have time to pray, grow their faith, and find the right help for them. I wanted others like me and Richard to have a chance.

I pondered this on the drive home with the bag of journals and books leaning against the back of my seat. I couldn't see them in my rear-view mirror, but I knew they were there, and it comforted me to attempt to check on them. My chest hurt, and my heart was racing so much that I subconsciously placed my hand on my chest most of the car ride home. I debated with myself whether I truly needed the journals. Should I just have left them in peace? Or were they meant to show me something from Richard? Tapping my fingers on my chest to the rhythm of my fast-paced heartbeat, I pleaded, *Please, show me somehow that this is okay or not okay.*

I arrived home, took my bag out of the car, and lugged it over my shoulder into the house. My husband and I ate dinner, and I told him a little bit about the books I'd found. After dinner, Cory and I decided to start thumbing through the books, which led to thumbing through Richard's journals. I transitioned from standing at the dining room table to sitting in our living room by the window with my computer in my lap and a few of the journals stacked next to it. I opened a document to take notes just in case something spoke to me. I searched some of Richard's sentences in Google, and most turned out to be fragments of quotes from famous writers. They weren't the gibberish we'd once thought they were. Learning this gave me hope.

Pages turned into journal entries, and Richard had written about a particular day when his best friend, Justin, had asked him to go surfing. He'd written about kicking a ball to a boy as he walked across the sand. He'd written about trying to surf over and over again, getting "worked" by the waves. He'd written about watching Justin surf. Then he'd written about God. Specifically, God walking on water. I felt that Richard was writing this memory because he'd been happy to have experienced it. He'd been thankful for his friend, Justin. At that moment, he'd been thankful for the waves and the sand and God. From his writing, I got the sense that this particular day with Justin had brought him peace and a flicker of hope amidst so much turmoil.

While I read the last few words of this journal entry, I felt a tingle on my right arm. I looked over, expecting for nothing to actually be there, and saw a ladybug crawling on me. In my home on a winter night, a ladybug was crawling on me. It quickly crawled to my back, and I jumped up, asking Cory to clarify that the creature was, in fact, a ladybug. My heart raced like earlier, but it felt different. This was adrenaline or excitement, maybe a little of both.

Cory tried to grab the bug as he clarified that it was a ladybug, but it flew down to my leg. I timidly walked over to our dining room and placed the palm of my hand beside the ladybug. It crawled onto my hand, and I brought it up closer to my face. I was stunned as I gazed at the ladybug, trying to talk to Cory at the same time. Its wings fluttered, and I could faintly hear them over my words.

I heard the flutter of its wings once again as it flew off my hand. Cory and I looked all over for it, but the ladybug was nowhere to be found. It seemed to have disappeared just as quickly and surprisingly as it had appeared moments prior.

After I gave up looking for it, I researched the symbolism of ladybugs. I read that a ladybug's spiritual meaning is closely associated with love, inner peace, harmony, renewal, and regeneration. If a ladybug is seen hovering in one person's direction while in the house, it is a sign of a soul mate relationship becoming blessed by the spirit.

My mouth dropped open. *Just like the butterfly landing on Cory in the meadow on the mountain*, I thought as I glanced over my laptop at him.

I was overwhelmed reading that information from Google, but still a little hesitant to believe the ladybug was a sign from Richard. The unbelievable is often so overwhelming that we have a hard time accepting what cannot be explained. I put my laptop to the side and began to search his journals again.

As I thumbed through the pages, a set of small leaves slid down the crease of the notebook. I grazed my thumb across one leaf, tracing its delicate ridges, careful not to break it. I noticed a small, heart-shaped one. Their brittle stems were still intact, so I tried not to move them. Despite my efforts, another leaf slid ever-so-slightly down the lined page and revealed a mark, brown in color, that stained the center of the page with a faint, cloudy spot shaped exactly like a heart.

How interesting it was that a journal left untouched for close to seven years kept these leaves intact for me to find one day. The leaves imprinted onto the pages they had been pressed between as another layer to ensure their importance would be remembered. To ensure that whoever came across them would know that they'd been there.

That's all we truly want to do—leave our mark on the world for our loved ones to remember us by. We want to leave love for them, and I think it's no mistake that Richard was thinking about love when he picked up this heart-shaped leaf and placed it in his journal. I grazed my thumb against the edges of one of the delicate leaves once more. I touched the heart-shaped stain on the journal pages. I traced the spine of the journal, pretending that I could actually reach out to Richard's own heart and touch it. I quietly said to Richard, *I will always remember you.*

CHAPTER 26

Razor Scooter

Before I investigated the attic and storage unit, before he wrote in the journals, before the Adderall took over, before we lost Richard, we were siblings who never imagined a life where the other was not there. Before the unthinkable became real, we were children. And I have the best memories of those two children together. Lessons are woven into all of the memories as I reflect back on them as an adult.

I was ten years old when scooters were all the rage for us kids. I rode my silver one, whipping past neighboring homes, ignoring stop signs, and refusing to go on the sidewalk. The cracks in the sidewalk had already flung me off my scooter multiple times because the tiny wheels couldn't ride over the smallest of obstacles.

I felt like I was gliding at top speed as I pushed the asphalt and then planted my foot on the base of the scooter, which wasn't even wide enough to fit the length of both my feet. I liked riding my scooter better than skateboarding or longboarding because I had handles to hold onto and a tiny metal brake on the back tire.

I also loved that the scooter wasn't motorized. That afternoon, Richard's friend was the talk of the neighborhood because he got a motorized scooter, and everyone wanted to try it. They zipped past me on my scooter, standing on the wooden platform, not working hard at all to make it go fast. All they had to do was push a button, and it lunged them forward down the road, reaching top speeds. I followed them, deciding that I wanted a turn on that scooter!

I had seen Richard ride it with ease. All the boys in the neighborhood had gotten a try, and I always wanted to do anything Richard could do. I tossed my scooter to the side, discarding it in the grass, and insisted on getting a try.

Richard's friend reluctantly explained to me where the brakes were on the handles, and instructed that I should not press them hard. He told me to ease into the brake handle. There was a red button just below it that would increase my speed. He mentioned that I shouldn't press that hard, either. I wondered how I would be able to pull that off, because the button looked like it only had two options: untouched and pushed completely down. There didn't seem to be an in-between.

Still, I acted confident as I stood on the scooter. I balanced myself as the kid got the scooter started up for me. In an instant, I was off! I zipped down the road, wind kicking up my curls and a smile growing across my face. I felt like everything around me was a blur, and I had no idea what speed I was going. It terrified me and thrilled me at the same time.

Eventually the scooter slowed like the kid had said it would, and I debated when to press the red button. My thumb trembled, hovering over the button and then finally pressing it.

I fully believed I'd pressed the button gently, but apparently, I pressed it really hard. The scooter surged forward suddenly. In my immediate terror, I pressed down on both of the brake handles. This halted the scooter immediately instead of gradually, and I went flying over the handlebars. I kept a grip on the handles until I decided that I'd better let go before the scooter got flung into the air with me. I didn't want to roll down the road with that thing!

My knees slammed into the pavement, and loose gravel punctured my skin instantly. I jumped up, and blood streamed down both my legs. Gravel was stuck in the gashes in my palms.

In this fight-or-flight circumstance, I flew without hesitation. I didn't stick around for my brother and the other kids to reach me to see if I was okay, and I didn't stick around to find out how bad my injury was. I ran the few blocks home and began sobbing to my mother. I was furious at my brother for not helping me, and when he finally caught up to me, he proceeded to tell our mom through his gasps of air and between my cries that I'd been gone before he could reach me. Richard claimed that my bloody legs running home had been faster than that motorized scooter ever would be.

Weeks later, Richard was playing around with my Razor scooter with his friends. He didn't have trouble with the motorized scooter like I did, and my ego was still a little bruised, so I was embarrassed to be around his friends. Because of this, I went in the house as they attempted tricks on the scooter. I'd seen them do so many tricks with their skateboards. I still had scabs and bruises on my legs, so I didn't want to be tempted to try any tricks he was doing.

A few minutes later, Richard's friends threw the front door open, almost knocking it off its hinges, and rushed Richard in the kitchen. Blood was gushing from a slice on his forehead. His friends reported that somehow—and no one would be able to reenact this if they tried—Richard had gone up onto a curve to do a trick, spinning the bottom of the scooter around on its axis—and fallen. The scooter had kept on spinning, and once Richard was on the ground, his head had been right in line with the spinning scooter. His forehead had gotten sliced by the side of the metal platform and instantly began gushing blood.

Though I was the youngest one there, I leapt into action, grabbing a dish towel hanging from the oven door handle. I pressed it onto his head and told him to lean back. I picked up our kitchen phone on the wall and called my mom and dad, who were both at work. I calmly told them what had happened and recommended Richard would need to go to the hospital for stitches. I also knew that the injury was not dire enough for me to call 9-1-1 before calling my parents. They rushed home and took us to the emergency room.

Under the fluorescent lights, we took turns holding Richard's hand as the doctor gave him his first set of stitches. In my childish mindset, I felt like I had saved him. I'd sprung into action, made the emergency calls, explained calmly what had happened, slowed the bleeding, and held his hand as he got stitches. As young as I was, sitting there next to the hospital stretcher, I knew that I would do anything for my brother Richard.

CHAPTER 27

Birth

After twenty-four hours of labor, they wheeled my hospital bed into the operating room. Cory was getting dressed in scrubs and putting our things in the recovery room while I was surrounded by fifteen or so nurses and anesthesiologists. As our doctor scrubbed in, I got help sitting up and scooting over to the operating table. I was barely able to move on my own, so the nurses draped my arms over their shoulders and pulled me forward. The anesthesiologist looked confused as the nurses told him I was having another contraction. The Pitocin had been turned off, but it was still in my system, setting off contraction after contraction.

There I was under the fluorescent lights, getting prepped for a C-section. I'd stopped dilating, and our baby was sunny-side up and not budging one bit. The pain medication had worn off, and a new dose in my epidural hadn't affected me at all, so the next option before having to go under during the procedure was a spinal block.

A nurse gripped my shoulders and hunched me over hers as I sat on the operating table. She held onto me, arms wrapped tightly around me, bearing my weight and my own grip, as I wrapped my arms around her back. As we held each other, my face burrowed into her shoulder, she talked to me gently, encouraging me, as her cheek pressed against mine. She kept me still and calm as the anesthesiologist prepped for the spinal tap and then began his procedure.

I was frightened because I had to keep my spine curved and still during contractions once he got started. It was the kind of frightened where I knew that I had to do this no matter what, that this was the only option and I had no way around it. So I would bear it because

I had no other choice. I wept the entire time, and I exhaled heavily into the nurse's shoulder as she consoled me and held me.

I don't know her name, but I will always remember her as my advocate in that bright room where it was easy to feel alone. I quickly realized the doctor doing the spinal block procedure was also teaching someone, and I felt like I was in a scene from *Grey's Anatomy*. I wanted to yell at him, tell him to hurry up, but I didn't want to aggravate the person who was in charge of injecting a very large needle into my spine. Judging by their conversation, the needle was already lodged in my spine even though I couldn't feel it, and the doctor was lingering, carrying on a conversation, while I had to stay perfectly still during another contraction.

I'll give him the benefit of the doubt: it probably wasn't in my spine for as long as it felt like, but after twenty-four hours of labor, while I sat there being scared about my first major surgery, I like to think that they could have cut me some slack. I noted that the doctor was the only man in the room because my husband wasn't allowed in just yet. I unapologetically thought that his being a man was probably why he seemed so unaware of the pain I was in.

The nurses laid me down, and after a few minutes, they poked my legs and hips to see if I could feel the cold tool. I could, so they waited a few more minutes and then tried again. Thankfully, I was finally numb.

Once the spinal block procedure was done, I got excited again. The glass door slid open, and a man covered in scrubs except for his eyes and hands walked in. I'd have known those blue eyes anywhere. Cory quickly walked over to hold my hand through everything, the lines at the corner of his eyes creased due to his smile behind his mask.

Tired but excited, we were finally going to meet the stubborn little boy whom I had carried and grown for forty-two weeks, the boy who hadn't budged during all of my hours of labor. He was comfortable, but we wanted to hold him out in the real world. I felt a tugging pressure, and the nurses talked to Cory and me about the steps of the procedure. Another anesthesiologist to my right was making sure I stayed numb, and Cory was to my left, our hands clasped tightly together. A blue sheet was draped below my chest to keep the bottom half of my body sterile for surgery.

I wasn't sure how something could happen very quickly and in slow motion all at once, but that was exactly how I felt in that moment. The surgeon said, "We are almost to him. Get ready, Dad, with your camera." Cory kept hold of my hand and stood up as our son was being born.

I heard the baby's cries, and tears instantly streamed down my face. Cory knelt back down, cupped my cheeks, kissed me, and said, "I love you." The nurse placed our baby on my chest for a few moments and then took him to clean him while they closed me up. Cory went with our son.

Of course, I stayed with the surgeon and nurses—I was open and numb from the stomach down. Shortly after Cory left the room, my body began to shake violently, and I turned to the side to vomit. Forgetting I was still open, I asked if they could sit me up so I could throw up, but of course they couldn't. One of the nurses held a bag next to my cheek as I tried to aim. The shaking was from the Pitocin, which they'd told me was a possibility, and I was concerned I was shaking too much for them to be able to close me.

"Honey, you are not shaking anywhere except the chest up because of the spinal block. Try not to fight the shaking or else you will be even more sore for recovery." The nurse continued to console me, placing her hand reassuringly on my shoulder.

Exhaustion consumed me and panic set in. I began to cry, telling her I was scared to go to sleep.

She said, "Honey, it's normal for women to sleep right now. You can rest your eyes. We are going to give you a little bit of blood now, okay? It's okay; we're just going to hook you up to some blood. It's really okay to rest."

I was scared to rest. Something felt off, but I was not quite sure what it was. I later learned that I was hemorrhaging, and they had to give me a blood transfusion.

From what I was told later, they got it under control quickly, and none of us truly realized it had happened until hours later when a nurse came to check on me and told me. They'd handled the situation very well and didn't frighten me. I was wheeled into the recovery room, where Cory was with our son, who was getting all of his newborn checkups and tests.

My son was then placed delicately onto my chest, and the nurses said they could finish his tests with him on me. They call this time the golden hour of bonding, and I had never been more in love and at peace than I was on that day with my son on my chest. I rarely thought about the surgery or how tired I was. I never thought about how monumental this moment was for him, for us. I just let myself live it. I was in the moment, pressing my nose into him and smelling his hair and rubbing my hand on his soft, wrinkly back.

Cory and I pointed out little things to each other. How our son had long hairs on his ears, like a wolf, and on his back; how cute his nose was. How comfortable he looked lying on me. After an hour or so, I looked at the clock, noting in my head that it was 12:30, just past midnight. I thought about how long my parents had been sitting in the waiting room to see me after surgery and meet their grandson. I thought about how tired they must have been, waiting late into the night.

They told us that our room was ready. Cory pushed our son's bassinet and the nurse pushed my bed down the hallway, being as gentle as she could every time she had to go over a threshold. As we went past a window, the sunlight grazed my arm and draped across the blankets. I exclaimed, "It's not past midnight, it's only past noon!" The nurse and Cory both chuckled. With everything that had been going on, the time of day we'd gone into the operating room had slipped my mind. I began to laugh with them, grasping my side because it hurt a little.

After we got settled in our room, we invited my parents to come in and meet their grandson. I told Cory to hold him and introduce him to them, finally telling them his name. We'd kept it to ourselves all nine months. With a quiet knock, my parents cracked open the door and entered.

Tilting our son up a little in his arms, Cory smiled and said what my parents had been waiting to hear for years: "I'd like you to meet your grandson, Lucas Richard." My dad's smile stretched from ear to ear, but he fell silent. My mom gasped, bringing her hand to her mouth. I didn't need words from them; I knew what this moment meant to them. I knew what the name meant to them too.

Cory handed over Lucas for my parents to hold him for the first time. That hospital room is where Cory and I became parents and my parents became grandparents. Under the fluorescent lights and the humming of my compression wraps around my legs, a new branch had sprouted on our family tree, beginning a new joy, a new unconditional love for us all.

Richard would have been honored to have his nephew named after him. He would have been proud to meet him that day too. He would have been happy to have a new chance for this legacy to be different.

I want Lucas to know that in that moment, on the day he was born, a new legacy began. A new story began writing itself. Although I wrote this story, my story, Lucas is and will always be the author of his own. He will get to learn all of the great parts about his uncle, the real reasons I wanted him to be named after him.

Knowing that my brother, Lucas's uncle, was not going to walk through our hospital room door, I later wondered what I would tell Richard if I could. I would explain that someone out there in the world needs to know that they can make it through whatever ails them. Tragedy can come no matter how hard they might try to prevent it, and they need to know that no matter what, it's not the end for them.

And so, if I could write to Richard, I'd tell him this:

Richard,

On this day, our family's new story began. This is when Lucas Richard, your nephew, was born. I want you to know that I am going to be the best mother that I can be to him.

I have learned a lot about life from all that I have experienced during your life and after you were gone. In turn, I will teach Lucas these things. I will show him unconditional love, empathy, and mountains. I will keep him safe, adventurous, and active. I will teach him about nature and trails and camping.

I will watch him experience the world before him. I will let him get dirt under his fingernails and mud on his shoes. And when the time comes, I will let him hike ahead a little on the trail. I will be close enough to always keep an eye on him, but far enough to witness him feeling free as he runs his hands through the leaves or blinks toward the sun.

I will show him the trails and mountains that healed me. I'll teach him that you loved them as well, and if only for a short time, they healed you too.

I'll also tell a joke or two. He will know about mishaps and clumsiness on the trails because there needs to be humor in life. He will know that he does not have to be perfect. He will learn about hope and resilience. Above all, he will learn that hope is where the love that still lingers in your absence lives. The most important thing I want him to know is to never give up on hope and love. They are fundamental, and with them, anything is possible.

Love, Your Sister
Ryan

CHAPTER 28

Rivers

I drive into the parking lot where I once imagined you as a park ranger. The sound of the rocks crackling under my tires lets me know I have arrived as the wheels roll through a crumbling, one-lane road. Yellow and black signs by the road caution drivers about the rushing water on either side. Large boulders covered in ivy stand just above the rushing water, and the sight always impresses me. I am always stunned that this view is right there in the parking lot before I ever start to head toward the hiking trail.

The dense forest encloses this pocket of roadway, and I feel secluded here. I turn into a parking spot and shift my red Jeep into park. Suddenly, for the first time all day, I think about bears. Of course, I picked a hike to do by myself in a part of the Shenandoah Valley where bears are the most common. Of course, I picked the only hike, White Oak Canyon, where I have actually seen a bear before.

Drumming my fingers on my steering wheel, I think how you can learn a lot about yourself when you go from talking about a solo hike to actually doing one. You can learn a lot when your anxiety kicks in and you think you should not have done this. You learn that you are terrified of bears. A part of me believes that you, Richard, will put things in my view for me to experience, and nothing will ever come to harm me here in the mountains because I have you watching over me. Another part of me believes that a momma bear would charge me if I stumbled upon her and her cubs, no matter if your soul says, "Hey, bear, stop!"

I decide to rely on fate and my knowledge of what to do if I see a bear. I know how to let a bear know that I am there before I ever get the chance to startle it. I search through my things and decide that a water bottle will be my tool. As I start out on the trail, I crinkle and bend the plastic water bottle, making a plasticky popping noise over and over again where the brush is thickest along the trail. I am giving any potential bear a chance to scatter off before they feel like they have to fight.

Five minutes later, my heart rate begins to calm even though I am putting in more physical effort. Ten minutes later, my confidence climbs again, and I think, *Hey, I can actually do this! I can't believe I was panicking before!* My stride becomes more confident. Fifteen minutes later, I am able to think about you again, which is why I am here in the first place.

After hiking a little while longer, I find a place to sit among the bugs along the river's edge. Leaning against a rock, I drape my feet down over a fallen tree and set my pink North Face backpack down, resting it beside my feet. The sun shines through the trees, creating twinkling patches on the surface of the river. The glistening light reflects up at me, and it makes me feel like I am meant to sit right here, in the sunshine. You have always made me see the importance of the patches of sunlight, even when they had yellow jackets in them.

The rushing water weaves its way in between the rocks, traveling down to where I started at the trailhead and past it, beside the parking lot and then beyond it. I think about these rocks and how they have been molded by the river's force and direction. At first glance, it can seem like the river is adjusting to the rocks, going around them. But if you stay a while (a long while) and look more intently, it is the rocks that over time are truly morphing to the river. This makes me think about this life … my life … your life.

I think about all the ways we have created goodness out of unimaginable tragedy. I think about your life, and even though I would much rather have you here, sitting against this rock with me, I want you to know that I have let your life teach me in ways I never thought possible.

I have chosen to make something meaningful happen in every avenue I can because of you. Because if I do not, losing you has taught me nothing. It would not stand for anything, and that is something that I will never accept.

Staring into the sun's reflection on the river transforms my mind like I am looking into a crystal ball. You have placed people and things in our lives that we need, and you have placed us into the lives of the people who need us. Like the mother who came across your photograph in the wee hours of the night, finding the *New York Times* article written about you. She begged you to help her, and she wrote the email. Later, Mom answered her phone call and talked with her.

You gave Dad the joy of running. I don't know how or when, but one day, Dad decided to go for a walk, and then he jogged, and then he ran. Somewhere along the way, running gave him a fight that he can win, strength to grow, and determination to live on. And he always dedicates his runs to you.

You gave Dad your college best friend, Chris. Chris will by no means ever replace you, but after you passed, he reconnected with Dad, and they've run together in marathons. Dad and Chris share running as a common outlet. During their first marathon together, Dad and Chris embraced as Chris crossed the finish line, and the two of them shed a few tears for their accomplishment.

They cried because they both ran in honor of a loved one who took their own life. You helped Chris when his dad took his own life, and you wore a suicide prevention bracelet to all your baseball games together in college. It's on your wrist in one of your senior baseball photos, when you knelt down on the field for the photographer before the start of a game. Dad was the one who pointed your bracelet out to me.

They cried because after running 26.2 miles through a city, something happened to them. How could it not, with all the training, hard work, determination, and physical and mental challenges that went into those 26.2 miles? Maybe they talk to you when they run or feel connected to you somehow. Maybe they feel your strength and encouragement spiritually. Those miles can transform someone's mindset, and emotions come to a head when the finish line is crossed. On top of that, they embrace each other, someone who understood why they began the race in the first place. Sometimes there is no other adequate emotion except to weep.

You gave Mom other mothers. I have felt from the very beginning that out of tragedy, something needs to be done. We all feel compelled to help people, but I don't think any of us feels that deeply rooted need to help others as much as Mom does. The energy from grief often times begs for action. It is scary to see just how many mothers have needed Mom as well, and who may need to read these words I wrote about you. It's frightening to know how many people are out there searching to be heard, understood. It's so important for people to be able to look at an article or book and know someone else out there understands, that they are not alone.

You gave Mom the gift of Gretchen. She is a medical professional who wrote a book that describes some of your mistreatment in it. She came back to the medical field after learning about you and has become proactive in making a change. She is Mom's sounding board within the medical field and gives Mom the encouragement to know that this mission is important. She reassures her that their advocacy is needed, and she sits with Mom and listens as a friend.

You gave us Alan Schwartz randomly and swiftly, the *New York Times* reporter who Dad happened to hear say the word "Adderall" on the television one day at work. Dad's ears perked up as he walked by the TV in the ski equipment room. He was back at work in January, only two months after you had passed away, and your birthday was lurking around the corner. Alan spoke, and I do not know what he said specifically, but it clearly made an impact, because Dad stopped what he was doing and spent the rest of the day figuring out how to email him. If you Google Alan's name or your name, you will see just how much that winter January day snowballed into this story of you and keeping your legacy alive to help others. Like I said, he came into our lives randomly and swiftly. It is more than any one of us could have predicted.

After the article about you was published, we were jetted off to New York City for *The Today Show* and then *The Dr. Oz Show*. It was all a whirlwind, a complete blur, to say the least. I was too numb with grief to enjoy the trip or really comprehend what we were doing there. All I knew was that those producers felt that your story needed to be told, so I trusted them and went along for the ride. If we had been there for any other reason—pick any option out of hat—I would have been inclined to brag a little. But that's not how life works. I couldn't reach into the hat and get a better reason to be there, so I didn't brag, and most people we knew only realized we'd gone to New York City when the shows aired.

You gave the medical field a new pair of eyes. Some of them, anyway. We cannot change everyone's opinion or perspective, but I know that you have affected some. If that changes how they approach treating people, if they slow down and really listen to the people they see, then you have done great things already. It will never be everyone who believes in all of this or listens, but for every individual who does, that means everything. It's another snowball effect: by helping those people, your story then reaches the people that those people reach. Families are healed, relationships are restored. It can be remarkable.

My desire in all of this is that the doctors who are in the same position your doctors were in will slow down and see everyone as a person and think about all of the possible alternatives before writing a prescription. Sometimes, of course, a prescription is needed. I am not antimedicine by any means. I am against rushing, and as a result, being careless. I know there are great doctors out there. You, unfortunately, did not get to meet those doctors.

Being vocal about what happened to you can prevent more Richards from happening, and I do not use that reference toward your name lightly. After all, this entire book is proof to the world that you truly are much more than what happened to you. I hope you see that. Even though you battled an addiction that completely rewired your brain and you could not get free from that, here and now, I do not see you as a drug addict or a medical patient gone incredibly wrong. I see you puffy and covered in layers during our snow duck day. I see you gliding across the mountain as you snowboard at Big Sky. I see you positioned at first base on your college field, knees bent, cracked brown leather glove open on your knee, your palm facing the sky. I see you in the ravine at Jockey's Ridge, wading through the marsh grass. I see you.

My hope is that each medical professional who has come to know you or had a part in your medical treatment (or maltreatment) sees you. I hope that if they are still practicing, they change their ways and slow down. If some never change, well, I hope they can't practice anymore. You have already put that in motion.

You gave me butterflies. The butterfly tattoo that is etched onto my ribs. The zebra-striped butterfly we went to see in the backyard, one of the last good memories I have with you. The black-and-teal butterfly that landed on my teal '66 Mustang. The butterfly field in the middle of a hike with Cory. The only black-and-teal butterfly in the meadow, who landed on Cory's hat, staying in place for a while, symbolizing you saying to me, *Here is the one for you.* Butterflies seem to follow me around, especially during the first summer that you were gone. When butterflies circle me or land on my hiking boots during a hike, I will always think of you.

You gave me Big Sky, the very place where my healing began. I carry so much of Big Sky in my heart every day because I know that's where your heart was most alive. It's where a lot of this book took place. I have already said so much about Big Sky, and I thank you for loving a place that allowed me to fall in love with it too. A place that gave me permission to heal.

You gave me hiking, my true north when I saw no other way in the dark of the night. When I found your love for the mountains, I ran to it and never looked back. Running in the pitch black of the night of my grief, closer and closer to my refuge. Healing takes time. Moving on takes courage, but I hold onto that one speck of light in the sky that represents them both, and I reach for it step after step. The night slowly turns into dawn as I find my way. When it gets light, I introduce other women to the mountains. Honoring you, I continue to invite other women along to hike beside me. Their sense of adventure continues to widen and illuminate my own path.

It's true that my life would not look like this if I did not have the loss of you to help shape me. There is something about a bruised person that appears more approachable, allowing friends and strangers to open up. I am thankful that I am approachable. I am even thankful to have been bruised so I can help others.

Now I can wholeheartedly write that I believe whatever someone may be going through right now, they can make something good out of something terrible. They can live on, and they can do it with meaning and heart. And even if it is hard, it does not have to harden them.

I have also discovered in the past couple of years that there are many things I have yet to unpack, things I have yet to deal with completely. This has not been a walk in the park by any means. You have taught and continue to teach me all sorts of things about life and how to live it. And because of you, Richard, I think that I have come to understand what life is all about. The list of what life encompasses continues to grow, but to me, it is about the moments that create our happiness.

To swing the bat and run the bases of my softball beer league no matter what parts of my body may be jiggling around. To swim in waterfalls and slide down natural rock slides, no matter the fear of bear-crawling up the rocks to the top of the slide in a bathing suit.

To always have more words spoken than left unsaid. To do things that help enrich others. Give with open hands. Write what matters. Write what will help others. Write out all of the words from the good and bad so others can relate and begin to unpack their hardships and use them to build hope.

To show love. See and experience new things. Always challenge myself to do what I am destined for. Find my calling and then give it away. Invite women to hike, and watch as they build strength and believe in themselves more and more. Be the person others can come to, but also have a person like that for myself. Be myself. No matter what, be that.

Do things that awaken something in me. Do the things that widen my eyes and make me feel strong, make me feel alive.

To be alive and truly live my life to its fullest—that is also what your death has taught me. Being alive gave me the opportunity to fall in love with the outdoors. Living to the fullest taught me to fall in love with the right person and nothing short of that. Healing taught me strength and resilience. Moving on taught me to climb mountains not because they are easy, but because they are worth it. Because when I summit a mountain, that is when I feel most alive. I imagine that's how you felt too.

That is why, to me, your life stands as tall as a mountain. I believe that you continue to have your hands in all this dirt that the mountain is made of. You take the dirt and shape it into a mountain for us to climb and overcome. You make your valleys become our lessons. Your weeds grow into evergreens. Your rain pours down and turns into growth for everything we touch. Our determination turns into sunlight. You turn your peaks into shared triumphs.

You also turn our tears into waterfalls that run down into rivers, touching everything, starting from the highest mountain peaks and coursing all the way down into the valleys. Then, when we did not know what to do with our grief, you turned us into those rivers. Rivers with an abundance of water to nourish life. Rivers that stem from one another and continue to spread out across the land to reach more life, dirt, wilderness, and people. Like rivers providing water to animals, we provide help to whoever needs it, shaping rocks into stepping-stones for others when the river becomes too wide and swift.

Richard, sometimes I want to scream at the top of a summit how much I hate that you are gone. It bottles itself in the pit of my stomach like water beginning to boil in a tea kettle. It slowly but then suddenly rises to the surface, and I want nothing more than to release it into the air. Fuming, boiling, and shaking, I want to howl a frenetic noise over the mountains and release the heartache permanently. But I know that it is in me for a reason, and screaming would only be a temporary release. Rather than the screeching of a tea kettle, or a maddening howl in the wilderness, I long to be a continuous rhythm, a knowing and calming sound to the human ear. A river that steadily flows down to reach and nourish everything in its path, a calm stream—and then, suddenly, a waterfall.

"A river," I say softly to myself and graze my thumb over these two words written in my journal. A rush of the stream spreads across the rocks and over my feet. I look up and see a group of hikers coming out of the woods in a single-file line and wading through the ankle-deep water. The water gives way to their legs, which ripples across the river to my feet.

One guy asks me, "How far is the waterfall from here? Are we going in the right direction?" I tell him which way to go and approximately how much farther they have. I also ask him which parking lot they parked in, because from experience, I know that there are two: one at the very top of the trail and one at the very bottom. I'd hate for them to hike to the wrong one. I smile and think of those deceiving fire roads from a few summers ago.

I splash my toes in the river, looking down again at the sunrays reflecting off the moving water. I feel glad to be a river. I feel glad to be *in* a river, when I realize this. I splash my toes one more time to find the appropriate way or time to say goodbye to this euphoric spot I found along the trail. A spot that now means so much to me.

Just like enjoying views from a summit, there is never a great time to leave. I may not be ready; I may not want to. I do my best to soak it all in so I can take this memory with me. I want to be able to keep it with me forever. The more I hike and the more I give myself these views and experiences, the more they become a part of me. And I have to acknowledge that there is a piece of me that is always a part of the mountains. I am a river, and it makes getting up and leaving rivers a little easier.

To everything there is a season.

—excerpt from Richard's journal

CHAPTER 29

A Decade

" What were you doing at the beginning of this decade?" Cory asks this simple question on our five-minute drive home from church. It's sunny, but the brisk winter air keeps our windows rolled up in our car. After all, the year and the decade are coming to an end in a few days, and we are entering a new decade. His is such an innocent question, but I had not quite put it into perspective for myself yet.

As I turn the blinker on, I manage to say, "Honestly, not to bring a negative light to your question, but the beginning of this decade was when we began losing my brother. I never expected that. Yeah, that's crazy to think about." And it was. In the fifteen seconds it takes me to pull into our driveway, the last ten years flash before my eyes. With more clarity now than I had ten years ago, I can use a better word to describe it instead of using the word "crazy." "Remarkable" comes to mind instead.

Earlier that morning, at church, the pastor had said, "We overestimate what we can accomplish in a day and tend to underestimate what we can accomplish in a year." *Let alone a decade*, I remember thinking to myself.

But how right he was. At the beginning of this decade, I was in the beginning of a hell I didn't yet know the depths of. No matter how hard it already was, I certainly didn't know that I would lose my brother a year and a half later. At the beginning of this chapter, I wrote that we "began losing" my brother, Richard. I use this phrase on purpose because it was an agonizing process that I always thought he would overcome. But instead, it came to an abrupt and unexpected end.

It would be hard to acknowledge when I was in the thick of it that it was not the end for me too. I was still there, picking up charred and disintegrated pieces. Within those pieces, I still had an entire life to go live. I just had to figure out how. I hope that these pages show you that it's possible. These pages are me figuring it all out. If you find yourself one day with grief barreling down the mountain toward you, I hope you know that healing can and should be done. I hope you know that there is more ahead for you, even if you can't see around the corner, the switchback, quite yet.

When you were in the depths of those valleys with me, I hope you knew that hope was and is always present. Hope is there like a best friend who never lets go of your hand. Hope will win. Hope *did* win.

If you found yourself spending time with my book because you are dealing with the depths of grief, I want you to know that there is always a way through. You can overestimate and become paralyzed by what you feel the need to accomplish in a day, week, month. Time's passing can seem like a cruel trick when it feels like you are getting further away from the life you imagined.

But you can also underestimate where you might be in a year, in a few years, in a decade. It's true that if you have lost someone, you will always be getting further away from the life that the person you are grieving was in. But if you let life do its work, and you do the work also, you will begin experiencing a lot more. More than you had imagined. And a decade later, you will see it all with a refreshed perspective.

You now know where I have ended up at this point in my life: in a loving home with a wonderful husband, two dogs, and our son, Lucas Richard. I am very far from perfect, but I like to think that makes this story relatable. I hope you feel like you are sitting down with an old friend who doesn't beat around the bush.

My family's legacy changed when Lucas came into the world. A new branch on the family tree sprouted, and that is where new life, new promises, new love began. And let me tell you: it's astounding that a decade later, here we are, somewhere I never could have predicted I would be, no matter how hard I might have tried.

My decade was process after process of getting me to this moment. After Richard passed, I went to the depths of our hell and spent years climbing back out again to experience much more than I'd ever anticipated. I am glad that I came through; I am glad that I was able to learn. I had no idea that I would be here, in this very moment, welcoming a new decade and saying goodbye to this one with so much joy and love in my heart.

In the ten years that have gone by, I lost my sibling after his two-year battle with addiction to prescription medication that completely and devastatingly changed almost every aspect of him—except for his love for nature. I believe that love of his stayed intact to be a lifeline for me. That one part of him created all of this, a true north and a direction for me to go in when I could barely see through the dark night of my grief.

I navigated the unimaginable while still attending school, getting a business license, and graduating. After that, I went to Big Sky and finally started the process of truly healing. I had a major breakup shortly thereafter, after spending five years with that person. But that freed me to dive head-first into healing the way I needed to and become healthy.

All those experiences, healing, struggles, and navigating it all—I know they got me ready to meet Cory, the love of my life. I fell in love with him quickly. He believed in me and helped nourish my love for hiking and camping. I hiked so much after meeting him, which inspired me to create a hiking group for other women out of pure passion and listening to my intuition. We got engaged and married. We honeymooned and hiked around Asheville, North Carolina. We went back to Big Sky with my parents, and I got to spend a week introducing him to the place that began this journey of healing for me. With every adventure, we grew and bonded, and I knew that Richard played a role in this.

Finally, and with so much more ahead of us, I gave birth to Lucas Richard.

These last few sentences written above are the cliff notes of my decade, because this chapter's purpose is not to rehash all of the details, but to celebrate where I have been able to root myself. If you told me eight years ago that I'd use the word "celebrate" ever again, I would have rolled my eyes and probably cursed at you under my breath.

But luckily for us all, it is now years later. I am a far cry from those years behind me, and I am proud of where my new roots are growing. I like to think that Richard would be smiling from ear to ear because of how I have picked up the pieces and made a life that he would be proud of.

Speaking of the life I created, the little baby boy we created, who is full of life, is currently with his Nana so I could go to a coffee shop and write these final words today. Missing him after spending an hour or so writing and reminiscing, I press Save on these final pages. I close my laptop and gather my things. I throw away my empty coffee cup and head out the door to my car across the parking lot. It's a rare sunny and seventy-degree day at the end of December, and I want to get back to my son and his Nana, my mom, so we can spend some time outdoors before the sun sets.

I walk into my childhood home and am greeted with the sweetest smile and giggles from Lucas in the living room.

I quickly put him in the stroller and head out the door so we can all go for a walk together. I have visited my childhood neighborhood and home plenty over the years, but I have not gone for a walk there in a really long time. It's surreal to me to be walking with my mom and my son up these streets and sidewalks where I once rode my bike and played hide-and-seek with the neighbors. Where I chased after my brother and his friends as they rolled around in trashcans, on bikes, skateboards, and scooters. They loved acting like they were on the latest episode of *Jackass*. As I thought about all of these fond memories, so many injuries flashed through my mind.

At the entrance to the neighborhood, we head across the street to the park at the church. I pick Lucas up and place him in a swing. He's not quite big enough for the baby swing, but he loves it anyway. Mom stuffs her jacket under him and wraps a blanket around his torso to secure him better. He looks like a stuffed snowball with arms and legs attached, grinning.

I give Lucas a light push and act like he's going to knock me over as he returns, backing up slightly and letting out a scream for him to react to. He laughs each time. Then I go to get his feet, and I tickle him when he returns over and over again. I'm smiling and take a personal note to remember these laughs, squeals, smiles, to remember pushing him in a swing on a mild December day. He reminds me to be in the moment; he reminds me to gasp and marvel at the simplest things.

I think about these past ten years, an entire decade, as I push him on the swing. I notice every quirk of a smile on the sides of his mouth and his glances up to the sky or over to his Nana. I think about those charred pieces I was dealt years ago. How they burned my hands, leaving scars that shaped me into the woman I am today, the mother I am today. The switchbacks and turns that I could not foresee ahead of me. The good. The bad. They were all of the moments that lead me here, to him.

After giving Lucas one last push, I pick him up. Squeezing him, I nuzzle my nose into his neck, so he leans his head onto mine, and I inhale everything that is sweet and kind, innocent and loving about him. I debate for a moment if I ever have to end this hug.

There is so much that I want to say to him as I hold him there. I come up with some thoughts that I keep to myself at the time because he is a baby, but I feel that they are important to share here now.

Lucas, I will help you live life to the fullest and have adventures. I am your home and safe place. I will hike with you to summits and guide you through all the twists, turns, and switchbacks along the way. Whatever obstacles you may face, I will always be here. I know I am here today to introduce you to the world and all its beauty. I know I am here today to take you on this journey called life.

When you are a little older and the trail widens into a field of butterflies, I will let you go ahead of me slightly. As I watch you wander ahead, gazing at the butterflies in the field and running your fingers delicately along the blades of grass, a teal-and-black butterfly will circle you. You will reach your hands high in the air for it to land on your fingertips. Once it does, your dad will come up beside me, wrapping his arm around me, kissing me on the cheek. I will bring my camera up to my face and press the shutter button, taking one frame, one moment captured, so that we can watch you hand-in-hand together.

In these next moments, I will watch the butterfly dance around your hands. As the sun shines upon your face, as the butterflies flutter about, as I watch you free and at home in nature, I squeeze your dad's hand and think of the last thing I want to tell you, Lucas.

I want you to know, Lucas Richard, that it's an honor to be your mother.

Acknowledgements

To God: I have learned that you work all things for good. You never let me go too long without working on my calling of writing this story before you would give me a nudge in the right direction. Proverbs 16:3: "Commit your work to the Lord, and your plans will be established."

To my brother, Richard: It's interesting to be at a loss for words now. My feeling that there is not much more to say is equal to my feeling that I can never truly be done writing our story. You wanted to be a writer and inspired me to pick up this dream and carry it through by writing our story. With tragedy came purpose, and although I'd much rather have you here, I want to thank you for entrusting me with carrying on your legacy in my own way. I hope that this book is something you can be proud of.

To my parents, Kathy and Ricky: You were the strongest force together as you supported me through grief when yours was barreling down on you too. I am forever grateful to you both for remaining steadfast and always being a beacon for me. You make me reflect on what it takes to have a lasting marriage in times of sorrow.

To my husband, Cory, my first book editor and always my biggest supporter: Thank you for believing in me and always encouraging me to push through to see this book come to fruition.

To my son, Lucas: I learned what kind of person I truly wanted to be when you were born. You are my inspiration, and I hope to show you that you can always try something new and have the faith that wherever you end up is where you are supposed to be.

To my in-laws, Pat and Kevin, for raising a wonderful man who supports and dreams with me.

To the DiSilvestro, Bemis, and Wentworth families, for being my best friends and becoming family; for being there during the best days in my life and the worst; for never letting go.

To the women of Her Hike Collective: Without you, *Her Hike* would not exist. You stepped out onto a trail with me, trusting me with your adventure. You opened up. You explored. You inspired me. I hope to continually return the favor.

To my editor, Christina Kann: I can't imagine anyone else editing my memoir. Your words were heartfelt, and you took great care in a story that meant the world to me.

To my proofreader, Mary-Peyton Crook: You refined *Her Hike* and were excited to work on it. Thank you for being enthusiastic during this process.

To everyone on the Brandylane Publishers team: Thank you for your hard work, edits, and design to get *Her Hike* where it is now.

To Brittany Latimore of Lines and Paint: Your art on the cover of my book was meant to be. I shared Richard's mountain sketch with you, and you made everything come together in a breathtaking piece of art.

To Dr. Siegel: Thanks for countless hours of your time and giving me a safe place to share all of my feelings and fears of the future; for helping me grieve and process.

To Alan Schwarz: Thanks for answering my dad's call and shedding light on the negligence my brother endured.

To the Board Members of the Richard Fee Foundation and to everyone who helps keep Richard's memory alive: Thank you for all your hard work, support, and donations year after year.

To Elizabeth Henson and Sharon Hundley: Thanks for always pushing me and telling me that I was equipped and meant to do this.

To S.A. Borders-Shoemaker and Emily Madison, two very talented authors who willingly read my writing: Thanks for my first rounds of feedback and giving me the push that I truly had something here to share with the world.

To everyone mentioned in my memoir: There are a multitude of thanks I could give to you all, but there are just too many of you to name. Know that whether you walked a lot of this journey with me or were only present for some parts, please know that you are seen, known, and loved.

To the readers: Thank you for finding *Her Hike* and taking it home with you; for giving it a space on your nightstand, coffee table, or bookshelf. The idea that you let my words take up space in your mind and heart is something that I will always be in awe of. The possibility that Her Hike inspires you to hike in the mountains and use what nature can offer you to heal truly makes me joyful.

About the Author

JESSICA R. CHENARD is a writer of purposeful adventures, healing, and legacy; hiking and writing give her a sense of creativity and purpose. She is a business owner, mother, wife, daughter, sister, community builder, and friend.

Chenard is the founder of Her Hike Collective, an all-women's hiking community. You can find her hosting the group's quarterly hikes in the Blue Ridge Mountains.

Chenard was motivated to write this book after spending a decade living it. She hiked to heal from tragedy, and later hiking helped her nurture a beautiful life. People she cared about played a large role in nurturing her love for the mountains, the most significant of these people being her brother. After his tragic death, she was left with only the knowledge of his love for nature and hiking. This enabled and inspired her. His love for the outdoors gave her a direction to go in—her true north—and she made hiking a part of her lifestyle. Ultimately, writing this book became her calling.

Chenard passionately believes that spending time in nature can heal. When you endure a tragedy or even just a hard season, hiking and nature can be a lifeline for you too, just like it was for the author. This story is written for you.

Lightning Source UK Ltd.
Milton Keynes UK
UKHW012134110722
405718UK00004B/80